FRENCH
COUNTRY
AT HOME

FRENCH
COUNTRY
AT HOME

Kathy Passero

Sterling Publishing Co., Inc.
New York

Published by Sterling Publishing Co., Inc.
387 Park Avenue South, New York, NY 10016

©2002 by Michael Friedman Publishing Group, Inc.

Distributed in Canada by Sterling Publishing
c/o Canadian Manda Group, One Atlantic Avenue, Suite 105
Toronto, Ontario, Canada M6K 3E7
Distributed in Great Britain by Chrysalis Books
64 Brewery Road, London N79NT, England
Distributed in Australia by Capricorn Link (Australia) Pty. Ltd.
P.O. Box 704, Windsor, NSW 2756, Australia

ISBN 1-4027-1000-3

Editor: Hallie Einhorn
Art Director: Jeff Batzli
Designers: Lindgren/Fuller Design
Photography Editor: Kathleen Wolfe
Production Manager: Richela Fabian Morgan

Color separations by Chroma Graphics
Printed and bound in Singapore by C.S. Graphics

1 3 5 7 9 10 8 6 4 2

To Peanut, for future travels unlimited.

ACKNOWLEDGMENTS

I am deeply indebted to the following people, all of whom contributed enormously to this book by sharing their insights and expertise with me: Heather Card, Cheryl Lynn Ernest, Ross Frances, Doug Karlson, Sally McConnell, Charlie Smallbone, Mark Steinke, Carole Winer, and Gay Wirth. A special thank you goes to Brunschwig & Fils for allowing me access to their extensive library and their showroom containing the Cabanel Collection. I am also profoundly grateful to Jean Renoux for giving so freely of his time and vast knowledge of French provincial furniture, which proved not only fascinating but invaluable to my research.

Next, I owe a most sincere thank you to my brilliant editor, Hallie Einhorn, for her flawless editorial instincts as well as her encouragement, endless patience, and her faith in me from the start. *Merci* also to my French tutor, Pascal Gharemani, for providing me with a perpetual connection to the French language and culture, and to my friends Sheryl Berk, Debbie Rosenberg, and Alyssa and Scott Shaffer for their unflagging moral support during this project.

Finally, my deepest gratitude goes to my parents, Virginia and Richard Passero, who read every word first—as they always do—and who introduced me to France so many years ago. Most of all, a warm and heartfelt thank you to my husband, Greg Dutter, who has shared so many wonderful visits to France with me and who continues to be the best companion I could ever hope to have, in travel and in life.

CONTENTS

❦

INTRODUCTION

◆◆

Whether it's a fisherman's cottage perched on a windswept cliff in Brittany or a centuries-old stone farmhouse in sun-kissed Provence, there is something irresistibly alluring about the French country home. Even the term "French country" conjures up a tapestry of romantic images—from a rustic kitchen anchored by a weathered trestle table laden with loaves of crusty bread, sausages, olives, and hearty red wines to a cozy retreat featuring a canopy bed and timeworn wooden shutters flung open to let breezes flutter through lace curtains.

Many of us find such visions so seductive that we hoard colorful postcards and calendars replete with images of lavender fields, ancient doorways framed by rose vines, and red-painted old-fashioned barges drifting peacefully past bucolic vineyards. Drawn by the idyllic rural lifestyle that these scenes suggest, we mount them on our bulletin boards, tape them to our computers, and dream about escaping our ordinary lives for a vacation—perhaps a permanent one—in *la belle France*.

For me, this passion for the French countryside developed almost twenty years ago, when I was a university student living in Paris. To expand our education beyond our course work, my fellow students and I were encouraged to visit historical sites in various small towns. My first excursion—to Chartres—proved so entrancing that I followed it up by exploring Honfleur, Blois, Saint-Malo, Les Baux, and a number of other intriguing places. Each time, perhaps to my

PAGE 8: *Drawing much of its inspiration from the natural landscape, French country decorating features an abundance of bright colors, earthy textures, and heady scents—all of which magically transport us to the bucolic regions of France. Here, rows of fragrant lavender create a bewitching sight on a sunny day in Provence.*

RIGHT: *The sun-dappled stone façade of a French bakery is awash in flowering plants. No detail seems to have escaped the owner's notice, from the hand-carved sign placed over the door to the charming statue welcoming shoppers.*

OPPOSITE: *Much of life in the French country home revolves around the dining table—a reflection of the casual, convivial lifestyle that prevails in rural France. This invitingly rustic room sets the stage for festive meals with friends and family. From its exposed wooden ceiling beams and terra-cotta floors to its sturdy wooden harvest table and rush-seat chairs, the space abounds in the earthy appeal of French country style.*

professors' disappointment, I was as enthusiastic about the intricately carved armoires, the fascinating *marchés aux puces* (flea markets), and the delicious crêpes and tapenade as I was about the cathedrals and châteaux. I took great pleasure in wandering through lively outdoor markets, strolling down side streets, talking with the owners of family-run auberges, and absorbing as much as possible of what seemed to be such an enviable lifestyle. I grew to love the curious old hotels with their crooked garret rooms, often brightened by floral-patterned fabrics and idyllic toiles de Jouy. I even developed a fondness for claw-foot tubs and the quaintly awkward handheld sprayers that substitute for showers. And I adopted a new morning ritual of a restorative bath followed by the comforting warmth of a bowl of café au lait or *chocolat chaud* (hot chocolate).

Over the years, as a writer living in Manhattan, I have returned to France as much as possible—for business and pleasure, first by myself and more recently with my husband to introduce him to the places that have given me such joyous memories. After each of my early visits, though happy to be home, I would find myself longing for something I'd left behind. So I became a passionate collector of anything that reminded me of France. I came back from Brittany and promptly hung a wrought-iron pot rack over my kitchen sink, loading it with slightly dented and tarnished antique copper pots, pans, and ladles salvaged from garage sales and antiques shops. I came back from Provence a year later and painted my dining room a deep bittersweet orange, then filled it with vibrant

RIGHT: *Known for their welcoming spirit, many French country rooms boast shades of orange, red, and gold. Here, apricot walls, burnished wood, and glowing candles beckon residents and guests to sit down at the table for a leisurely meal. The mood is sophisticated, yet never so formal that a faithful pet would be shooed out of the room. Note how well accents of blue complement the warm backdrop.*

Provençal-print fabrics and pottery that I had lugged home in an extra carry-on bag. Suddenly, I found that just walking into my kitchen and glimpsing the soft glow of old copper or sitting down at my dining room table whisked me back to favorite moments from my travels, buoying my spirits in the process.

What is there about the French countryside that makes us yearn to bottle a bit of it and bring it home to uncork and savor whenever our souls need nourishment? Part of this phenomenon comes from the joie de vivre that embraces rural France. The countryside is a place not only where vibrant colors, heady aromas, and mouthwatering cuisine prevail but also where—despite the encroachment of ATMs, American-style fast-food chains, and the world's ever-accelerating pace—much of life revolves around simple quotidian pleasures and a robust appreciation for them. People still visit neighborhood butchers and corner bakers to find the freshest ingredients for lunch and dinner. They still spend long, congenial hours at the table, lingering over delicious dishes, fine wines, and interesting conversation with friends and family. Men still play *boules* (bocce) in the sun-dappled

LEFT: *At the other end of the same space, elements of the classic French country kitchen merge old-world charm with contemporary style. Neat as a pin yet full of interesting touches, the setting features such provincial favorites as a* crémaillère *(pot rack) hung with gleaming copper cookware, a stash of woven baskets, and blue-and-white ceramic tiles. Other fitting accents include an antique wire birdcage and a small sculpture of two rabbits resting quietly on a shelf beneath the island. Animal themes are another common motif in the French country kitchen.*

parks on warm afternoons, and parents still take their children to sail charming toy boats in fountains.

Of course, all this hardly suggests that residents of rural France don't lead busy, active lives. They do. But they also have a way of indulging in life's little joys, making even the most basic elements of daily life seem like small luxuries. Take the simple French breakfast of a steaming bowl of café au lait and *tartine*, for example. *Tartine* is, in essence, just buttered bread with jelly. But when you savor the crusty, golden baguette with sweet, creamy butter and fresh orange marmalade, the experience is worlds away from drinking instant coffee out of a Styrofoam cup and wolfing down a processed muffin that came wrapped in plastic—a routine that many of us engage in every morning.

As you will see in the following chapters, French country architecture and interior design capture the essence of this approach to life through their convivial warmth; their abundant use of rich colors, vivid patterns, and varied textures; their celebration of natural materials; their emphasis on family and history;

and their tendency to display eclectic, often whimsical accents. At once sophisticated and relaxed, provincial homes envelop their residents in comfortable, livable elegance.

Perhaps the most appealing aspect of French country architecture and decor, though, is the fresh, spirited originality that they demonstrate. While there are many design hallmarks—which we will explore in the coming chapters—there are no rigid guidelines. Rather, the style encourages you to put your own unique spin on the decor, using whatever aspects please you most. Venerable antiques are free to mix with new items or quirky flea-market finds, and accents from different regions are invited to rest side by side. What's more, you don't need to embark upon an all-encompassing French country scheme to reap the benefits of the aesthetic. Something as simple as draping a kitchen table in a sapphire-and-maize tablecloth or stocking French soaps and bath oils in a woven basket on the edge of the tub will bring a hint of Gallic flavor to your home.

That's where this book comes into play—to help you incorporate French country style into your own home to whatever degree you wish. In Part One, we will examine the basic hallmarks of French country design, breaking the style down into its individual components: the distinctive architectural features; the energizing colors, textures, and patterns; the lovingly handcrafted furniture built to last for generations; and the personalized, often quirky accents that pull a space together—all the cornerstones you need to bring the magic of the French countryside to your residence.

In Part Two, we'll take an evocative room-by-room tour of the French country home. We'll peek into the bustling rustic kitchen to explore its undeniable appeal, stop for an entertaining gathering and a hearty dinner in the living area and dining room, venture into bedrooms and baths to bask in their pampering comfort and coziness, and step out to the patio for such delightful outdoor pastimes as gardening and plein air dining.

Think of this book as a departure point—a source of information and inspiration that will help you unlock your own imagination, whether you plan to refurbish your entire home or simply add a bit of French country panache to a favorite room. Choose whatever images and suggestions strike a chord with you, and blend in ideas of your own. The goal is to create a beautiful, comfortable environment that you will enjoy. Once you have achieved such a setting, take the time to savor it. After all, doing so is a crucial part of *l'art de bien vivre*—the art of living well.

OPPOSITE: *Highly versatile, provincial decorating schemes mesh easily with other styles. In this eclectic vignette, a Greek Ionic column sits between a sofa covered in upholstery reminiscent of a Turkish kilim and an armchair with a matching ottoman, their sunny yellow color and dainty pattern calling to mind the mini-prints beloved in Provence. All of these pieces blend seamlessly with a modern window treatment and walls textured to evoke the mottled shell of an old country farmhouse that has stood the test of time.*

PART ONE

DESIGN HALLMARKS

◆◆

CHAPTER ONE

ARCHITECTURAL DETAILS

Amble along any country lane in France, and you will soon come upon a charming rural home. Depending upon which region your stroll takes you through, this dwelling might be a venerable stone farmhouse with a doorway framed in tumbling roses or a tidy whitewashed cottage trimmed with brilliant blue shutters. Then again, you might encounter a tall, half-timbered abode crowned by a rustic thatched roof and graced by window boxes brimming with scarlet geraniums.

Architecturally speaking, there is no quintessential French country–style home. Rather, there are dozens of styles, each with its own unique design hallmarks, and each indigenous to a different region. Just as every French province boasts distinctive culinary specialties and cultural treasures, each has its own traditional methods of constructing homes.

RUSTIC FAÇADES

Indeed, as you travel from region to region, the architectural landscape changes. Alsace-Lorraine, for example, is dotted with medieval villages of brown-and-white half-timbered houses featuring pitched roofs, gabled windows, and flourishes of colorfully painted gingerbread trim that make them look as though they might have been lifted, *Wizard of Oz* style, from the mountains of neighboring

PAGE 18: *Fortunately, you don't need to live in France to enjoy the refined rusticity of French provincial homes. By incorporating such architectural elements as a large stone hearth and terra-cotta tile flooring, you can achieve a French country flavor in your own residence.*

RIGHT: *With their time-honored half-timbered construction, these homes in Alsace speak of old-world charm.*

OPPOSITE: *A vine-covered stone manor house in the Loire Valley boasts dazzling blue architectural accents. The French passion for color often manifests itself in the form of vividly painted shutters and doors in hues ranging from creamy lavender to brilliant crimson.*

Germany or Switzerland and set down on the French side of the Rhine River. This similarity in architectural style is hardly a surprise when you consider that the region belonged alternately to France and Germany through much of its history. (It finally settled into a permanent home as part of France during the last century.) Naturally, the German influence wove its way into Alsatian architecture just as it did into Alsatian cuisine, the latter being a robust marriage of French and German tastes, with sauerkraut and the hearty meat-and-potato stew known as *baeckeoffe* among the favorite dishes.

By contrast, peek out a window in Provence and you'll spy a jumble of ruddy terra-cotta tile roofs protruding at odd angles like shards of lovely broken pottery. Supporting most of these are thick, rough-textured stone walls, often covered with either a bright white lime mixture—to keep rooms cool by reflecting the blistering Mediterranean sun—or a layer of ocher. Over the seasons, the sun's rays fade the ocher to softer hues; reds mellow to rosy pink, browns to creamy café au lait, and yellows to soft fawn.

Not surprisingly, most provincial architectural traditions evolved over the centuries in response to practical considerations. One such factor was the availability and cost of building materials. People in the countryside generally constructed their homes from whatever natural resources were close at hand, plentiful, and affordable. Thus, you find limestone in the homes of Normandy, granite in Brittany, and clay and wood throughout the country. "Half-timbering was the early way of building houses in Normandy, Burgundy, Alsace, even the Basque country because there was so much wood available," notes historian and

LEFT: *Age and the elements are responsible for the appealingly weathered look of this venerable home in Provence. The ruddy ocher shade of the façade is typical of the region, where houses often draw their palette from the natural landscape. Battered wooden shutters keep out the oppressive summer heat, but can also be flung open to usher in cheerful sunlight.*

designer Jean Renoux, who leads tours and seminars on French architecture and culture through his company Art & Architectural Tours. "The timber frame was filled in with whatever people could find—clay and straw, mud and small stones, or other materials. Some beautiful examples from the thirteenth and fourteenth centuries still exist."

Weather was another important factor in the development of rural architecture. In the Alps, where winter brings heavy mountain snowfalls, slanted roofs have been customary for centuries; the angles are gentle enough to allow a layer of snow to accumulate as natural insulation, while the rest tumbles off rather than building up dangerously as it would on a flat roof. Along the northern coast, the use of water-repellent stucco over stone became a building tradition to keep the lashing rains and ocean winds at bay.

History, too, has affected architectural forms. In Burgundy, for instance, it is not uncommon to spot colorful glazed tile roofs of the style often associated with Belgium, though the region is nowhere near the border. The technique actually dates from the Middle Ages, when Flanders—before joining the Hapsburg empire—became, for a time, the property of Burgundy's powerful dukes. Trade and travel between the two areas naturally increased, with Flemish craftsmen introducing their traditional roofing technique to the Burgundians.

Of course, the French countryside is also home to grand summer residences, manors, and hunting lodges once belonging to the nobility, as well as magnificent châteaux in regions such as the Loire Valley. But by and large, provincial

OPPOSITE: *Despite its somewhat distressed façade, this French country estate boasts a pristine look with its orderly rows of multipaned windows accented by white-painted shutters. Provided there is no structural damage, the owners of old French country homes often leave signs of weathering untouched.*

ABOVE: *Terra-cotta roof tiles, a whitewashed façade, and sky blue shutters give this cottage its quaint appeal.*

LEFT: *A cluster of terra-cotta roofs juxtaposed against verdant hills forms a picturesque skyline for this village in Provence. To brace against the mistral, the ferocious wind that blows for as many as 150 days each year, Provençal houses almost invariably face south or southeast and feature only tiny windows on their northern exteriors.*

dwellings are simple inside and out, lacking elaborate columns, gargoyles, or carvings. They were originally the homes of farmers who tilled the soil, vintners who tended the grapes, and other working people who were poor in the worst of circumstances and of modest means in the best. The appeal of these homes lies not in elaborate architectural detail but in their rich testament to the past and to the lives of the people who lived in them.

HOME AND HEARTH

While the façades may differ, French country interiors share a number of architectural features that fill them with character. From low-ceilinged farmhouses in Bordeaux to chalet-style cottages tucked away in the Alps, rural French dwellings greet those who enter with a welcoming sense of warmth and rustic comfort.

Most homes dating from the nineteenth century or earlier were originally built as a single large communal room where family members would eat, sleep, and spend what leisure time they had. (As owners became more prosperous, they simply added rooms.) The focal point of this central space was a massive fireplace, or *cheminée*, which not only provided the means of cooking but also acted as the home's primary source of heat. It could be constructed of flagstone,

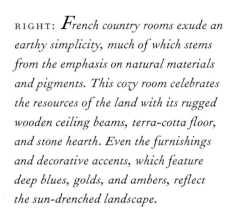

fieldstone, clay, or brick, depending upon the region. Today, the hearth continues to hold a place of prominence in the home, though its walls and surround have most likely become blackened with use over the years. With a crackling fire blazing from within, the *cheminée* is as serviceable as ever, encouraging residents and visitors to pull up a chair and warm their toes.

Additional architectural hallmarks imbue French country rooms with old-world appeal. Overhead, you are likely to find exposed wooden beams making their mark against a white-painted ceiling; sometimes the beams are left plain, while other times they are whitewashed or stained and varnished. Closer to eye level, antique mullioned windows, casement windows, weathered wooden shutters, and doors bearing their original ironwork infuse living spaces with time-honored charm.

Perhaps the most notable aspect of the French country interior is its emphasis on natural materials: stone floors, terra-cotta hearth tiles, and timbered ceilings abound. Their presence conveys an earthy ruggedness, a sense of living close to the land. Those homes built before or during the nineteenth century also tend to evoke a sense of history, which gives them a solid, reassuring quality as well as a feeling of timelessness. Each seems to tell an intriguing story—as if the spirits of

the house's many past residents are still present, the countless conversations and celebrations held over the years almost audible. New generations of owners tend to cherish this aura of history. They preserve ancient timbers rather than plaster over them, exalt a worn fieldstone floor's patina rather than scrub it away or replace it, and harbor a fondness for every chink and curious angle into which the house has settled during its long existence.

SETTING THE STAGE

Happily, there are many relatively simple ways to bring the flavor of French country architecture into even the most modern of rooms. The best place to start is with the interior shell of the home. Rough-hewn faux half-timbering, for instance, can be added to a ceiling to evoke a fairy-tale setting. In a similar vein, an ordinary Sheetrock wall can be coated with stucco to create a wonderfully coarse backdrop reminiscent of French provincial designs. You could also open up a wall with French doors leading out to a flower-filled garden. Doing so will give your space an airy feeling while welcoming in much-appreciated natural light. The floor is yet another surface that can take its cues from age-old French country practices. Laying down uneven flagstones, for instance, will transport residents and guests back to an era when stones were collected by hand and carried from the field, no two alike in size or shape. The same tactic could be applied to a fireplace for a similar effect. Since the hearth tends to be a focal point, its style will have a powerful impact on the overall mood of the room. Another possibility would be to affix a decorative nineteenth-century mantel to a wall.

When it comes to the more service-oriented rooms, such as the kitchen and bath, Provençal tile can step in to make the spaces as beautiful as they are functional. Opportunities abound, from counters to backsplashes to tub surrounds. Such tiles could also be used on a patio to establish a French country tone. Any of these options will heighten a space's visual interest and lend it handcrafted charm and individuality.

To achieve a French country ambience, you can use either contemporary reproductions or actual reclaimed antiques. A number of companies in both the United States and Europe specialize in vintage doors, shutters, mantels, stone flooring, hand-painted tiles, and other architectural elements salvaged from historic French churches, monasteries, farmhouses, country schools, carriage houses, and barns. Such items are quite durable—after all, they've survived for more than a

OPPOSITE: Terra-cotta tiles, a golden textured wall treatment, and French doors can inject French country style into any setting. Here, such elements combine to create an uplifting, sunny milieu. Luxurious curtains accented by tasseled tiebacks pitch in to add panache.

century already—and, in some cases, surprisingly affordable. "Antique French terra-cotta tiles actually cost less than new hand-molded ones," notes Doug Karlson, president of Country Floors, a New York–based company that has specialized in reclaiming specialty tile from Europe for nearly forty years.

By contrast, antique doors, shutters, and mantels may require a substantial investment, but these offer homeowners the opportunity to incorporate exquisite, one-of-a-kind items into their living spaces. And the quality of these architectural elements is unrivaled. Mark Steinke—managing director of Salvage One, a twenty-year-old Chicago company specializing in architectural reclamation—has found gems ranging from four-hundred-year-old doors with their original hand-wrought castings to spectacular casement windows rescued from an orangerie on the grounds of a château in Bordeaux. Steinke makes at least eight trips to the French countryside every year to hunt for architectural treasures; he uncovers some at antiques shops and auctions, while he finds others hiding in farmers' barns, where they have been gathering dust for more than a century.

As you glance through the photographs in this book, make a mental note of the architectural elements you find most pleasing and those you think you could most easily incorporate into your home. If possible, start with empty spaces so that you can better study the "bones" of each room. (Often, it is difficult to visualize structural changes in a fully decorated room.)

Remember that you needn't overhaul an entire room to achieve the desired effect. Subtle touches and individual elements that draw the eye can evoke rustic charm just as effectively. Floors, walls, and woodwork in rosy browns, mellow beiges, and other shades that convey a sense of warmth will successfully set the stage for any French country furniture and fabrics you plan to add. You might also replace elements of brushed steel, chrome, and other man-made substances that convey a sleek, contemporary aesthetic with stone, rough-hewn or polished wood, and other natural materials. If you are hesitant to make dramatic changes, start with temporary "trial" items. Place a pair of tall terra-cotta pots on either side of the fireplace to decide whether you really want to cover it in antique terra-cotta tile. Line a kitchen counter with a set of cheery blue-and-yellow ceramic Provençal canisters before you decide to retile the counter itself. Such simple measures will give you a feel for the ultimate effect without committing you to a substantial investment.

OPPOSITE: *The distressed paint finish on the cabinets and dishwasher in this French kitchen suits the rustic backdrop. Rooster motifs—a common theme in French country decorating—enliven one pair of cabinet doors, while copper pots hanging from a* crémaillère *(pot rack) reflect the warmth of their surroundings.*

ABOVE: *Golden glazed tiles form a practical backsplash that seems to melt into the wall above. A narrow line of accent tiles contributes a bit of visual excitement and provides a link to the green cabinetry.*

CHAPTER TWO

COLOR AND PATTERN

A primary attraction of French country style is the feeling of warmth and conviviality it exudes. Much of this ambience comes from an abundance of rich, lively colors and patterns. A table might be layered in not just one radiant Provençal print but several—glowing orange over bold crimson topped with luminous gold. A red-and-white toile de Jouy might brighten not only a bedroom's comforter and pillows but also its curtains and walls, inspiring dreams as elaborate and vivid as the fabric's detailed pastoral scenes.

In southern Provence, the unofficial capital of French country style, interior design draws its inspiration from the sun-drenched landscape. The intense blue sea and sky, green olive groves, and fields of dazzling yellow sunflowers find their way into many a home, creating a sense of unity with the natural environment and bringing a touch of the outdoors inside. To walk into one of the countless little fabric shops in Avignon or Aix-en-Provence is to marvel at how such a visual cacophony blends into a harmonious whole. Tablecloths, place mats, linen napkins, and other treasures crowd every counter and corner. Here, a pattern of plump golden pumpkins on a fiery auburn background looks perfectly at home next to a sapphire cloth adorned with bunches of chartreuse grapes and meandering vines.

Americans, in general, shy away from such exuberant colors and patterns. Instead, we tend to favor items that are understated and matched—an entire dining room set of the same furniture, for example, or place settings in which every piece of china, from soup bowl to dessert plate, features the same pattern.

"When people see all these bright, lively colors, they fall in love with them," says interior designer Cheryl Lynn Ernest, who owns a French country shop and decorating business in Chagrin Falls, Ohio. "They are a breath of fresh air after the toned-down neutrals and safe colors of the 1990s."

Of course, not every French farmhouse overflows with color. But even the most basic fisherman's cottage often boasts a splash of it—say, a pair of brilliant Breton blue shutters enlivening a gray stone façade. In other homes, texture provides the visual intrigue. A weathered wooden trestle table on a pocked stone floor yields a neutral color scheme yet still conveys a sense of rugged warmth. Similar to the way in which a golden, crusty baguette with butter can be just as satisfying as the most sumptuous meal, these earthy interiors—whose beauty lies in their natural simplicity—have just as much to offer as their more lavishly decorated counterparts.

A COLORFUL PAST

The French countryside's love affair with color and pattern dates from the mid-seventeenth century, when thanks to improved navigation, ships began arriving from India bearing, among other exotic goods, brightly printed cotton fabrics. The French had never seen such spirited colors and designs. Even better was the fact that the new imports could be washed without fading. The whole country went wild for what came to be known as *indiennes*. Soon everyone from the Paris court to the peasantry was dressing in imported cotton and draping beds, chairs, and even walls with the cheap, hard-wearing textile.

The newfound fabric so eclipsed silk, linen, hemp, and wool that French factories found themselves on the brink of ruin. To quell riots and calm mill owners, King Louis XIV banned the import and domestic manufacture of *indiennes* in 1686. The plan backfired, however. As contraband, the cloth became even more coveted, fetching astronomical prices on the black market.

It wasn't until 1759 that France lifted the ban, acknowledging that there was a fortune to be made in producing *indiennes* domestically. It took several more decades and a little espionage for French manufacturers to master the age-old Indian art of creating colorfast dyes and using carved wooden blocks to hand-stamp or "block" the cloth. When they finally did, they added their own distinctly French colors and design motifs. By the late eighteenth century, *indiennes* were a national fashion symbol.

RIGHT: *A collection of riotously colorful throw pillows features toile de Jouy and Provençal prints—both signature elements of French country style. The flamboyance of these accents is particularly striking in the middle of this contemporary setting, which is bathed in creamy ivory and white. Adding another dash of provincial flavor is the chunky pottery in shades of gold and amber.*

The most famous factory to emerge from this era was run by a Bavarian named Christophe-Philippe Oberkampf in the town of Jouy-en-Josas, near Versailles. Oberkampf developed a technique of printing single-color patterns—usually red or blue on a white background—consisting of pastoral and mythological scenes (elegant ladies and gentlemen of the court on garden benches, peaceful countrysides with grazing cows, and so on). This style of fabric, known as toile de Jouy (cloth of Jouy), became a favorite of Marie Antoinette and later Napoléon. The workshop closed after Napoléon's reign ended—around the same time that the hand-blocked *indiennes* fell out of favor. The waning popularity was due in part to the Industrial Revolution, which put small manufacturers out of business and led to inferior-quality production-line design.

A century later, a French family named Deméry started collecting antique fruitwood blocks, opening a fabric factory in Terascon, France, in 1938. Soon the factory name changed to Souleiado—an old Provençal word to describe the sun shining through the clouds after a rainstorm—and the firm became the leading maker of modern *indiennes*. Souleiado's designs are inspired by the forty thousand priceless carved blocks stashed in its archives, and—in true French fashion—every imperfection, chip, and crack is replicated to add character and historical accuracy. The company's fabrics first gained popularity in the United States when Pierre Deux imported them, and today a handful of American shops operate under the Souleiado name, importing fabrics from the Terascon factory. Happily, quite a few French companies now produce equally lovely traditional-style *indiennes* (among the best-known is Provence's Les Olivades), and a number of shops and catalogs make them available in the States.

LEFT: *Toile de Jouy, often simply called toile, has experienced an enormous resurgence in the United States during recent years. Perhaps part of its appeal lies in the escape from chaotic modern life that the delightful country scenes seem to promise. Here, a toile in soft shades of moss green and white is mixed with plaid and floral prints bearing the same cool color scheme. Using muted pigments prevents the combination of patterns from appearing overly busy or jarring and instead suggests an aura of restraint and understatement.*

ABOVE: *Boasting a long-standing tradition in French country decor, lace continues to be a favorite fabric, particularly for window treatments. This lace curtain pairs amicably with a red-and-yellow toile valance against a weathered window frame. A still life of sweets, fruits, and fresh flowers completes the pretty picture.*

PAGE 42: *Deep russet paint imbues this cozy dining area with a feeling of warmth. While a coarse texture gives the windowed wall plenty of visual interest, a stenciled leaf pattern lends the smooth wall a touch of panache. Notice how the swag at the window ties the scene together with its pattern of meandering vines.*

Of course, you needn't restrict yourself to *indiennes* or toiles to capture a French country mood. Lace, too, makes a charming provincial adornment. While the dainty-looking fabric was invented in Italy during the 1500s, it became a specialty in Normandy by the late 1600s. Lace curtains, bedspreads, and tablecloths graced many a stylish home in the 1700s and 1800s, and today these delightful accents remain French country favorites, particularly in the north.

Even more formal, sumptuous textiles once reserved for the wealthy—such as silk jacquards and damasks, petit point embroidery, Aubusson rugs, and tapestries—can work well in a French country setting. A pair of apricot damask drapes, for example, can be paired with a sofa upholstered in a bright orange-and-yellow Provençal print to lend a touch of sophistication to any living room.

HARMONIOUS BLENDS

To embrace French country style, you will need to vanquish hesitations about dramatic tones. Rather than ivory tablecloths paired with subtle gold-rimmed ivory china, think scarlet, burgundy, and sapphire. Of course, this doesn't require turning your home into a Crayola box of wild color. Start by browsing French country shops and perusing magazines, catalogs, and websites. If you have the good fortune to travel to Provence, pop into some of the charming shops selling *tissu* (fabric) and *linge de table* (table linens).

Make a mental note of the color combinations and patterns that speak to you. Though they may look randomly assorted, most contain a unifying element. A room might abound in patterns, yet closer inspection may reveal that the florals, fleurs-de-lis, and paisleys are all variations of a vertical stripe—some wide and bold, others slender and delicate.

French decor often draws comparisons to the much-praised French sense of fashion; the guiding principle for both is harmonizing rather than coordinating precisely. In lieu of a living room set, the French country gathering area is apt to boast several disparate chairs and sofas that together create a unique expression of the owner's personality. "A lot of my clients are locked into the match mindset; I encourage them to break free and throw together whatever they love," says interior designer Cheryl Lynn Ernest, whose shop operates under the Souleiado name. "Invariably, they find that something connects the items." Understanding this concept liberates you tremendously in terms of decorating.

FABRICS AT YOUR FINGERTIPS

In addition to the classic French country fabrics of toile de Jouy, lace, and the cotton prints known as *indiennes,* the following six textiles and textile-design techniques are often used in French country decor. Below is a brief primer highlighting the basic features of each.

Jacquard actually refers to a type of loom, invented by Joseph-Marie Jacquard. A social activist, Jacquard became so concerned by the terrible conditions endured by child laborers in French textile mills during the 1700s that in 1805 he designed an automated loom. His intent was for this device to replace the young workers and end their suffering. The machine used perforated cards to create intricately woven designs that could be made quickly and with minimal labor costs. Jacquard looms became enormously popular and are still used in the manufacture of many fabrics, including damasks, tapestries, and brocades. Today, the term "jacquard" is used more loosely to describe fabrics of intricate weaves or patterns.

Damask is a weave that alternates shiny and matte finishes to create a reversible fabric. It was first produced during the fourth century in the city of Damascus and was later introduced to Europe by Marco Polo during the thirteenth century. Originally made exclusively in monochromatic color schemes, it now comes in multicolored designs and can be woven of almost any natural or synthetic fiber. Patterns include everything from paisleys and florals to animal motifs and harlequin diamonds. Damask is often used to evoke a sophisticated look for curtains and upholstered furniture.

Brocade is similar to damask, but bears raised patterns—resembling embroidery—that are created by adding a greater number of threads to the weave. Originally gold and silver were favored, though today brocade comes in any number of colors, decorative motifs, and fabrics. Like damask, it is a favorite for elegant, traditional interiors.

Chinoiserie refers to a decorative style that became fashionable in Europe after Marco Polo's return from the Far East. The style increased in popularity as merchant ships brought goods from exotic ports during the sixteenth century, and it has stayed in vogue ever since. Used for fabric, wallpaper, porcelain, and other decorative elements, it reflects European artists' wildly imaginative visions of Asian life, often mixing elements of Indian, Chinese, and Japanese cultures by conjuring elaborately whimsical scenes of pagodas, elephants, monkeys, geishas, and so on. Chinoiserie is most often duotone, but can be multicolored.

Petit point features hand- or machine-embroidered pictorial designs, usually stitched over a pattern stamped onto fabric. The technique became de rigueur for well-bred women in the sixteenth century. It was—and still is—used most often for chair seats and backs.

Chintz is cotton fabric busily printed with flowers, fruit, and other motifs, and sometimes coated with a thin layer of resin for a slightly shiny, dirt-repellent finish. It is somewhat similar to Provençal cotton prints, though it is achieved through roller-printing—as is toile de Jouy—rather than hand-blocking. This process creates a pattern that covers the entire fabric surface as opposed to having a stamped design appear at specific points on a solid background. Chintz is a popular choice for curtains, table linens, and upholstered furnishings. (In England, it is also a favorite for china patterns.)

Once you've identified favorite color schemes, consider setting the stage with lively walls. A room painted bordeaux or bittersweet becomes more dramatic and less traditional, not to mention snug and congenial. As an alternative to solid color, opt for wallpaper in a cheerful yellow-and-teal Chinese-inspired print or a crisp blue-and-white toile, both popular French country motifs.

For a touch of whimsy, you might try a trompe l'oeil (literally, "trick the eye") design. This style of painting, often depicting a landscape or a still life, is deceptively realistic-looking. Developed in Italy during the Renaissance, the technique caught on in France in the seventeenth century. Trompe l'oeil not only helps to add depth and dimension to an interior but also allows you to introduce elements for which you do not have room. For instance, a small kitchen might feature an entire wine-cellar vignette to give the illusion of cavernous space; a dining room might "open onto" a painted tropical garden, inviting the visitor to escape into a lush hideaway; and a study might be adorned with faux wood

BELOW, LEFT: *In this whimsical example of trompe l'oeil, a painted pig lolls blissfully under a "table" while such clever faux touches as a wine bottle, a bundle of garlic, and a pheasant blend effortlessly with real produce and bunches of hanging dried flowers.*

BELOW, RIGHT: *Under a kitchen cabinet, a trompe l'oeil plant created with tile seems just as full of life as the real plant sitting next to it. The butcher-block counter and the porcelain canister with its French label further infuse the diminutive corner with a provincial flavor.*

paneling to simulate the luxurious style favored by the aristocracy during the reign of Louis XV.

For these effects, you'll need to hire an artist or, on a less expensive level, an art student. Ask the staff at home decor stores for recommendations. Before any work is done, discuss the project in depth with the artist and present detailed examples of the look you hope to capture. It's wise to ask the artist to complete a small area for your approval before committing to a whole mural.

Other wall-brightening options include a stenciled pattern (perhaps a quaint fleur-de-lis at chair-rail level in a dining alcove), touches of decorative molding that speak of old-world elegance, or a textured paint treatment—perhaps rag rolling to simulate a Mediterranean fresco's patina. Don't forget ceilings and floors—buttery yellow overhead enhances the warmth and reflective glow of saffron walls.

After you've selected a wall treatment, you can begin to add an assortment of colorful, complementary fabrics, from curtains and upholstery to tablecloths and bed canopies. Layering patterns and colors often takes a bit of trial and error. One simple way to begin is by choosing two or three favorite hues—say, blue, gold, and red—and selecting items in colors that range from faint pastels to brilliant saturated shades of the trio. An alternative is to incorporate various patterns that bear flecks of similar colors. For instance, you could upholster a

RIGHT: *You needn't own an eighteenth-century manor house to surround yourself with historic charm and patina. Here, a trompe l'oeil molding steps in to lend a doorway a bit of character. For a humorous touch, a nesting bird has been painted to rest on the lofty perch. Note how the incorporation of subtle shadows makes the faux elements appear more realistic.*

OPPOSITE: *The French are masters at combining different patterns, colors, and textures for a harmonious effect. The key lies in finding a common element, as demonstrated in this sitting area, where toiles, plaids, checks, and stripes are united by their crisp black-and-white color scheme. A floral-print toss pillow adds a softening dash of pink, reinforced by the fresh cut flowers on the table.*

RIGHT: *A skillful blending of coordinated textiles gives this dining area its welcoming look. While the specific patterns vary from fabric to fabric, the general palette of red, blue, purple, and white remains the same. As a result, the various design components, from the chair upholstery to the layered tablecloths (the latter being a hallmark of French country decor) seem perfectly at home with one another.*

OPPOSITE: *An upholstered chair off to the side picks up the border of the upper tablecloth for continuity. Overall, the botanical motifs lend the setting garden airs, providing a strong sense of connection to the verdant outdoor area visible beyond the French doors. A flower-filled pitcher and two large stone eggs with speckled surfaces that seem to echo the crackled finish of the diminutive side table upon which they rest extend the theme.*

sofa in a Provençal print featuring a mustard background dotted with tiny green-leafed primroses. Then you could drape a rich crimson-and-gold paisley throw over the sofa. The reds and yellows woven through both fabrics should connect the elements and create a riveting tableau.

Don't hesitate to mix old and new. Find some of your treasures in catalogs, and search for others in flea markets. Squares of vintage lace can be attached to a sash rod over a kitchen window and paired with a pot of bright red geraniums to whisk you to Normandy every time you glance up. From a frayed green toile curtain, you might salvage enough material to cover a trio of throw pillows in different shapes. Placed on an emerald comforter, they would look elegant enough for a French king's hunting lodge.

Decorating *à la française* requires abandoning conservative, cautious notions and, instead, letting your passions guide you. The more you embrace this concept, the more vivid and lively both your imagination and your decor will become.

◆◆

CHAPTER THREE

FURNITURE

Picture yourself in a delightful French country kitchen on a glorious morning. Sunlight floods in through open windows overlooking a quaint cobblestone street or perhaps a flower-filled courtyard. Breezes laced with lavender, apple blossoms, or crisp sea air mix deliciously with the tempting aroma of café au lait. A hot cup of the eye-opening beverage awaits you next to a buttery, golden croissant.

While the details of this imaginary scene will change from person to person, invariably at the center of the vignette is a generations-old, rough-hewn wooden table. Despite the encroachment of modern appliances, the sturdy piece of furniture seems perfectly comfortable in its surroundings. Elsewhere in the house, the table's antique cousins—perhaps a cozy nineteenth-century *lit-clos* (box bed) or a distinguished four-poster—get along equally well with younger companions. Far from incongruous or outdated, these long-treasured furnishings look as handsome as they did when they were new.

French country furnishings hold a timeless appeal. Though there are myriad forms, from whimsically painted Alsatian cupboards to exquisitely carved Norman armoires, these pieces are unified by their irresistible combination of beauty and unpretentious functionality. Such furnishings might well be museum-quality, but nothing about them seems aloof or demands admiration from afar. On the contrary, they exude the warmth and welcome of items designed to be touched, needed, and used on a daily basis.

PAGE 48: *Formal furnishings often share space with more rustic pieces in French country interiors. Here, a weathered-looking cupboard seems right at home next to a graceful upholstered armchair and a dainty Louis XVI—inspired writing desk. An elegantly distressed design on the walls ties the scene together.*

ABOVE: *A distinguished armoire presides over this room, which is filled with elegant furnishings including a dramatic golden fauteuil and a painted daybed. However, the refined tone of these pieces does not prevent a more casual table with a curvaceous wrought-iron base from taking up residence in the space. On the contrary, the setting seems to benefit from this airy counterpoint.*

OPPOSITE: *The adjoining room brings the outdoors in, with its bank of windows, sunny yellow upholstery, and flower-filled urns. Terra-cotta tiles heighten the garden room tone, while an informal ladder-back love seat contributes to the relaxed mood.*

No matter how delicately an eighteenth-century craftsman chiseled decorative scrollwork into the façade of a buffet, he built the drawers, doors, and hinges to be hardy, knowing the piece would become a cherished family heirloom handed down from generation to generation. Today the nicks, dents, and patina that have come from years of use and countless fingertips brushing the wood surface only enhance an antique's appeal, lending it a sense of history and evoking a nostalgic feeling for a simpler, bygone way of life.

RIGHT: *This cupboard's chipped paint and nicked surface are testaments to its many years of service. Fluid carvings enhance the furnishing's appeal, while chicken-wire panels contribute a refreshingly primitive note. Currently employed to store and display a collection of prized linens, the piece is as sturdy and functional as ever. Having stood the test of time, it makes a statement of permanence and solidity.*

OPPOSITE: *An impressive Louis XV cherry* buffet à deux corps *dating from the nineteenth century is put to good use as a showcase for a magnificent collection of French majolica. Juxtaposed against this focal point are a petite chest and a diminutive upholstered chair, both of which cause the massive piece's grand proportions to become magnified. This practice of incorporating furnishings of different scale within a single space is common in French country interiors.*

A BRIEF HISTORY

French provincial furniture came into its own only about two hundred years ago. During the Middle Ages, furnishings were built directly into homes—a board for a table and slats for beds, secured in the supports of a humble one-room dwelling. By the 1700s, some of the common folk in the countryside and small villages had a few basic freestanding pieces—perhaps a table, a bed, and a few chairs. It wasn't until after the French Revolution that a middle class arose and farmers, merchants, and others became prosperous enough to start amassing fine things.

In fact, until the second half of the seventeenth century, even the wealthy had some limitations regarding furnishings: it was the custom among the rich to own a single set of furniture and cart it along from residence to residence—hence, the French word for furniture, *meubles* (movables). Louis XIV, the Sun King, was the first to demand a set of furnishings for each of his palaces. He also did much to position Paris as a center for excellence in design. Not only did he hire an arbiter of taste, but he also insisted that artisans and craftsmen adhere to strict guidelines—all of which were based on his own personal preferences regarding everything from waistcoats to writing desks. By the end of the 1600s,

OPPOSITE: *French country decorating often involves mixing pieces from different historical eras, as demonstrated in this sumptuous living room. Furnishings include an eighteenth-century Louis XV walnut armoire, nineteenth-century faïence urns from Provence, and a Louis XIII settee, all of which come together to create a warm and inviting setting.*

LEFT: *French country furnishings can feature beautiful carvings, as shown in this close-up view of the armoire. From the elliptical medallions on the door panels to the various vine motifs to the nesting pair of lovebirds above, the intricate work of the artisan engages the eye. Notice how the verdant ivy crowning the handsome piece recalls the leafy designs below.*

virtually every piece of furniture built in Paris was in the ornate Louis XIV style, full of lavishly carved details, veneering, and elegant inlay.

Indeed, French kings dictated design to such an extent that the country's various historical furniture styles bear the names of these rulers. Louis XV in the mid-1700s ushered in an even more elaborate look called rocaille, with lighter, more delicate curving lines and an abundance of shell-like designs, as well as gilding, painting, and marquetry. (The style is now often referred to as rococo, a term coined in the early twentieth century.) With the ascension of Louis XVI, neoclassicism came into vogue, and designs moved away from extravagant flourishes to simpler, straighter lines and ancient Roman and Greek motifs—trends accentuated in the subsequent Directoire and Empire styles.

Naturally, the styles set by the court filtered down to provincial furniture makers. Some visited Paris to study the leading workshops' techniques and bring them home; others were traveling craftsmen who crisscrossed the countryside, setting up shop temporarily with each client. But unlike the trend-conscious, court-controlled Parisians, rural artisans often mixed elements of different styles they liked, now and then embellishing pieces with a particular regional touch they had picked up. Part of provincial furniture's charm comes from this unique blending of designs.

History, geography, economics, and politics all influenced furniture design. Normandy, for instance, is renowned for its marvelous carving, a tradition that dates back to the Vikings, who lived in this coastal region around the 700s and, though better remembered for destroying than creating, were master carvers. Bordeaux's furniture reaped the benefits of the region's famous vineyards and port; much of this furniture features gorgeous mahogany inlay, courtesy of the countless wine ships that sailed to South America and returned bearing the exotic wood as cargo.

Such factors also led to the creation of distinctive pieces of furniture in certain areas. For instance, a specific type of chest—designed to hold the cocoons of silkworms—comes from the Massif Central in Languedoc, where people made a livelihood raising these creatures. From Auvergne comes a unique low chair, which was used by women making lace in that region. "Such pieces of furniture are very interesting because of what they tell you about the culture and the history of an area," notes historian and designer Jean Renoux. "However, they are rare and difficult to find in antiques shops today."

Like materials for building homes, woods for furnishings were chosen based on what was cheap and abundant. Périgord, for example, boasts vast walnut

forests. Not surprisingly, the majority of the region's furniture is carved from walnut. Mountainous Alsace, Savoie, Haute-Provence, and parts of Dauphiné, by contrast, favored fir and spruce. As pine tends to be an inferior-quality wood, painted furnishings became popular in areas where it was used heavily. "A lot of people today like the blue pieces; those come from Catholic areas, since that was the color associated with the Virgin Mary," says Renoux. "Depending on where you are, though, you can find beautiful examples of everything from geometric motifs like chessboard squares to stars and doves."

To a French farmer, vintner, or fisherman living in the eighteenth or nineteenth century, buying a piece of furniture was a significant—perhaps once-in-a-lifetime—event. Each furnishing would be discussed at length in advance and then handcrafted to match the purchaser's needs. Often, a tree from a farmer's own land would be chosen and chopped down to make the piece. Much of the furniture was commissioned for special occasions, weddings in particular. Because

ABOVE, LEFT: *Two rush-seat ladder-back chairs—classic components of the French country home—offer sun-splashed perches for weary residents and guests. Along with terra-cotta tile flooring, rough-hewn beams, and a vintage metal birdcage, these modest pieces add a hint of French farmhouse charm to the setting.*

ABOVE, RIGHT: *The practice of painting pine furnishings gave artisans broad canvases on which to unleash their creative talents. In the spirit of that tradition, this country cupboard boasts an array of delightful designs, including such French motifs as the rooster and fleur-de-lis.*

of this sentimental significance, such pieces boast tremendous appeal. It's almost as if a bit of the original owner's personality was captured in every timeworn wooden panel. One can imagine young children helping to polish the doors of their great-grandmama's armoire while listening to the story of how the treasured family heirloom was made—and how the anxious bride-to-be peeked in eagerly each day to inspect the furniture maker's progress.

AT HOME

There are a number of sources for French provincial furniture, from antiques shops dealing exclusively in items from rural France to roadside *marchés aux puces* (flea markets), where dust-covered diamonds in the rough await intrepid travelers. Even merchants at humble outdoor stands will often ship items around the world. You might consider taking a shoppers' tour of France, led by an expert who will guide you through antiques shops, factories, and flea markets, advise you on quality, and help you negotiate prices.

Another option is to look through stores and catalogs that specialize in authentic-looking reproductions—complete with distressed and flaking paint. A

RIGHT: *Contemporary French country–style furnishings that take their cues from time-honored designs fill this dining area with old-fashioned charm. At the center of the space, four coordinating ladder-back chairs pull up to an unpretentious pine table that recalls the farmhouse furniture of the Haute-Savoie. A cleverly distressed paint treatment successfully replicates the endearing weathered look of antique pieces, while the decision to alternate between furnishings bearing painted and natural finishes treats the eye to a bit of variety. Off to the side, a pine buffet with swag aprons and turned legs rounds out the tableau.*

FRENCH FURNITURE: A CONCISE GLOSSARY

berceau: cradle or crib

bibliothèque: bookcase

bonnetière: tall, narrow cupboard used for storing bonnets; most often found in Normandy

buffet à deux corps: two-tiered cabinet with a bottom section featuring doors and often drawers, and a top section consisting of two or more doors

buffet-bas: long, low cupboard or sideboard usually used to store dishes; called *dresche* in parts of northern France and Belgium

bureau: desk

canapé: sofa

chaise: chair

chaise de bébé: high chair

coffre: trunk or chest

commode: chest of drawers

encoignure: corner cupboard

enfilade: long buffet

guéridon: pedestal table

horloge de parquet: grandfather clock

lit: bed

lit à baldaquin: canopy bed

lit-clos: box bed enclosed with wooden panels, often hung with curtains to keep drafts at bay

lit d'ange: bed with four short posts over which a canopy is suspended from the ceiling

lit de repos: daybed

lit en bateau: sleigh bed; literally, "boat bed"

miroir mirror

panetière: cagelike wooden box with four legs and a grille in front, usually of turned wood; once used to store bread

pétrin: small box resembling a chest on legs; once used to hold rising dough

secrétaire: writing desk

vaisselier: tall cabinet with doors and drawers in the bottom section and open shelves on top, usually used to hold dishes

number of these companies also stock rustic pieces made by contemporary rural artisans who work in the French country tradition, crafting such items as rush-seat chairs and colorfully painted chests. Often, these furnishings are more affordable than their vintage counterparts. Reproductions also offer a greater variety of options and the opportunity to obtain furnishings that are tailored to your needs, such as queen- and king-size beds (virtually impossible to find in antiques) and matched sets of tables and chairs.

How does a first-time collector choose the right pieces? Start with what you love and will use. "I urge every one of my customers to go back to the root of these pieces—the utilitarian aspect," says Gay Wirth, who with her husband, Warren, founded New Orleans' Wirthmore Antiques, specializing in French country antiques, nearly twenty years ago. "French provincial furniture was

entwined in the daily life of its owner. These pieces have a heart and a soul—they're not just furniture, they're works of love—and they are happiest when they're used."

If you adore reading by the fireplace, a logical acquisition might be a wonderful nineteenth-century fauteuil, perhaps reupholstered in a bright yellow-and-orange Provençal fabric. If cooking is your passion and you often invite friends over for casual dinners, you might opt to incorporate a stunning *encoignure* (corner cupboard) or *enfilade* (long buffet) into the dining room, where you and your guests can admire it regularly.

You need not worry about a piece's original purpose, period, province of origin, or even scale. The charm of French country style lies in its eclectic nature, its limitless potential for mixing and matching and finding innovative uses for items. An exquisitely carved Louis XVI chair with a bit of patina can look striking next to a rustic pine armoire. A *panetière* once used to hold fresh baguettes might take on a new life as a magazine rack, and a *pétrin* that held rising dough a century ago might be revitalized as a charming chest for a child's sweaters or as a decorative cache for guest towels. The more you trust your instincts and let them guide you, the more you will enjoy your home—a secret the French have known for years.

A simple course of action is to find one wonderful piece and build a room or vignette around it. A massive armoire, for example, might dominate the end of a hallway; leave the door open a tad to reveal a collection of antique ivory linens.

Naturally, prices for French country furnishings vary a great deal depending on quality, condition, provenance, and availability, among other factors. Before you buy, spend time browsing. Ask questions, and keep a small notebook handy to jot down thoughts about what you like; include every decorative touch that strikes your fancy, whether it be a ceramic pitcher full of lavender serving as a centerpiece for a farmhouse table or an antique bed dressed with crisp blue-and-white linens to match its charmingly faded paint. Never feel intimidated to ask "rudimentary" questions; even the most knowledgeable antiques dealer started from scratch, and most will be more than happy to discuss their favorite subject with a fellow enthusiast.

OPPOSITE: *Although this bedroom is sparely furnished, it exudes the warmth associated with French country interiors, thanks to its terra-cotta tile flooring and its creamy ocher-toned walls. A graceful settee holds pride of place in front of the hearth, where it makes a powerful impact. Prominently positioning one or two cherished furnishings in a room while keeping surrounding elements to a minimum can be a rewarding way to showcase your favorite pieces.*

CHAPTER FOUR

◆◆

ACCENTS

To infuse your home with French country charm, you needn't overhaul your current decor or invest in large, costly pieces. A few carefully placed accents can communicate the style remarkably well, establishing a subtle French country ambience that will permeate your residence. A gesture as simple as placing an antique copper canister filled with wooden cooking spoons on a counter or clustering a few colorfully labeled bottles of calvados, Normandy's famous apple brandy, on a windowsill will add a dash of French country flavor to a kitchen. In a living room, stationing a pair of dried-flower topiaries on a rustic mantel will make a quaint French country statement. And topping off a bedroom nightstand with a small basket of thyme-and-rosemary sachets, wrapped in colorful printed cotton fabric, will inspire dreams of the fields of Provence.

Accents such as lighting, window treatments, artwork, and collectibles provide some of the best opportunities to express your personal sense of style. If you love antique glass, you might design a memorable vignette for a bathroom counter with an assortment of vintage French perfume bottles. If rich colors are your passion, you might drape your living room windows in grand, floor-length plum-and-vanilla brocade curtains paired with delicate lilac sheers.

Because French country style is itself so eclectic, it blends easily with other types of decor. You can borrow from different time periods, mix ornate and rustic items (pair a duo of simple ladder-back chairs with an opulent striped damask

PAGE 62: *Two simple yet endearing depictions of barnyard animals lend a touch of farmhouse charm to a corner that already abounds in French country appeal, from the crisp red-and-white toile wallpaper to the towering topiary and airy French doors.*

RIGHT: *Potted plants find their way into virtually every room of the provincial home. Tucked in among the colorful blossoms of this little indoor garden are such interesting touches as a small gold birdcage and an antique china box.*

OPPOSITE: *French country blends beautifully with other decorative styles to produce memorable interiors. In this romantically feminine hideaway, a toile tablecloth complements china dishes worthy of a traditional English tea, while an Italian armoire stands tall between two large windows. Note how the wallpaper, with its vertical floral pattern, echoes the painted designs of the statuesque piece.*

sofa, or set lavish gold torchères against coarse stucco walls), and introduce elements of other ethnic styles. "I've mixed French country with contemporary, American country, English country, and Italian. It works beautifully with other styles to create an old-world feeling," says interior designer Cheryl Lynn Ernest. The vibrant colors and patterns favored in French country make it a natural match for exotic items such as Persian carpets, Turkish kilims, and Italian majolica, while its rural roots make tokens of rustic Americana look right at home, too. A set of nineteenth-century rug beaters or potato mashers—bought for a song at a flea market in the heartland and beloved for the individual pieces' charmingly distressed wood finishes and unusual shapes—will add a nostalgic hint of farm life in much the same way that a priceless eighteenth-century French armoire would.

In choosing decorative accents for your home, select whatever you love, even if the items seem dissimilar. Chances are that when you arrange them together in a room, you will discover a number of common threads that weave through all of your favorites and give them a sense of unity.

BELOW, LEFT: *Lamp bases crafted from burnished woods are favored for the gentle warmth they lend interiors. Note how this polished base accentuates the subtle glow of the lamp.*

BELOW, RIGHT: *In lieu of harsh overhead lighting, chandeliers set the stage for cozy, convivial evening meals. To vary the look of your dining room according to the season, you might purchase a second set of small shades in a contrasting color or pattern.*

OPPOSITE: *A pair of slender brass lamps makes an attractive accent for the top of a small dresser. The muted auburn of the lamp shades adds a hint of color and enhances the warm gold and brown tones that dominate the furnishings and decorative accessories.*

Soft, reflective light is one of the hallmarks of French country style. Everything is aimed at evoking a sense of warmth—the flicker of candles shining against a gilt mirror frame, a cozy fire crackling in a gigantic stone fireplace, an elegant chandelier casting a romantic glow over an intimate table set for two.

Harsh, glaring florescent bulbs are shunned along with track lighting and other modern, gallery-style approaches. In fact, chandeliers often provide the only form of overhead lighting in French provincial houses. And as many American travelers have found when trying to read in French hotel rooms, bulbs tend to be of a lower wattage than in the United States.

To capture the comforting glow that pervades French country interiors, scatter three or four reading lamps on small tables around a room. Try using "soft" rather than "standard" white bulbs, switch from one hundred to sixty watts, and turn off overhead lights. To heighten the effect, consider lamp shades in hues of rose, gold, or other rich jewel tones. And when it comes to bases, materials that convey warmth—wood, brass, and ceramics—are preferable to cool, sleek

substances such as chrome and aluminum. Placing copper, silver, or gold accents near small lamps will help to magnify the sense of reflected light. For example, you might fill a polished copper teapot with wildflowers or dried herbs and place it behind a lamp, or put the lamp itself on a gleaming silver tray. Finally, nothing gives rooms a more inviting feel than candlelight. Line a mantel with ivory candles, use an assortment of tapers as a centerpiece, or let a fragrant votive on a hall table or bathroom sink greet guests.

FLOWING FABRICS

Windows provide an abundance of opportunities for inventive accents. A simple early-nineteenth-century Breton cottage might feature just a few small panes (with none facing north, into the wind), while a stately manor house in Bordeaux might boast a combination of quaint dormers and tall casement windows. Curtains for the former home might consist of the simplest white lace or printed cotton squares peeping out past painted wooden shutters, while those for the latter would probably involve flamboyant curtains hung high on the wall, embellished with rope-twist bullion fringe, and left long enough to puddle luxuriously on the floor.

Although there is no definitive French country curtain style, fabric is favored over venetian blinds and modern, minimalist window treatments. Likewise, translucent sheers—called *voilage*—take preference over pull-down shades. Unlike American sheers—which tend toward white and solid pastels—*voilage* often reflects the French passion for vivid hues and patterns. It is quite common to find gaily patterned undercurtains paired with heavier drapes in dramatic color combinations. For instance, to create a sophisticated look, black-and-white checked curtains might be set off by semitransparent ebony sheers dotted with tiny white fleurs-de-lis.

Edgings and tiebacks provide stylish finishing touches for window treatments. From tassels and fringe to braids and smooth ribbon, the possibilities abound. Even the hardware itself, from curtain rods to rings, can make a decorative contribution. A little girl's bedroom could include pink-and-cream toile curtains with feminine rosettes fashioned out of extra fabric to accent each pleat. A wine lover's dining room could express a touch of casual whimsy with sage curtains and claret sheers suspended from wrought-iron rings, each in the shape of a bunch of grapes.

ABOVE: *An ornate panel of antique lace makes a gorgeous treatment for a multipaned window. The scene becomes all the more picturesque when the curtains are left slightly open to reveal a window box full of pink blossoms that seem to be clambering for a peek inside.*

RIGHT: *Dramatic red-and-white floral curtains stretching all the way to the floor draw attention to an alluring alcove. At night, the scarlet tiebacks can be removed and the drapes drawn to guard against drafts and ensure privacy. During the day, a little writing desk positioned to make the most of the courtyard view offers a quiet spot to catch up on correspondence or simply daydream.*

ABOVE, LEFT: *A trio of timeworn glazed ceramic vessels makes an eye-catching vignette.*

ABOVE, RIGHT: *A sturdy old mustard crock finds a new role as a convenient receptacle for whisks and wooden spoons next to a jar of* herbes de Provence *and a distressed stone planter. In the Gallic kitchen, where improvisation and imagination flourish, what could be more fitting than finding innovative uses for old favorites?*

OPPOSITE: *An antique French barometer makes a fine pièce de résistance for a hallway. Small, simply appointed areas like alcoves and entryways often prove to be ideal venues for showcasing unique items such as this.*

COLLECTIBLES AND BEYOND

Perhaps the best part of decorating comes *after* you have completed the basics, when you can indulge in hunting for the little treasures that make a room feel like home. Virtually any memento can find a place amid French country decor, be it a special painting of the Côte d'Azur purchased during a vacation on the Riviera or an array of old candy tins amassed through years of combing flea markets. Build your decorative accents around your interests—not what you think will match your furnishings. Even something as seemingly misplaced as modern sculpture can look striking against a provincial decorating scheme.

Glance through books, shops, and catalogs for items that catch your eye. You might even discover a French twist on a favorite pastime. For instance, a sailing enthusiast could devote a shelf or mantel to replicas of the toy boats that French children sail through fountains in the Luxembourg Gardens. A cooking buff could purchase a wrought-iron pot rack and display copper pans and colanders rather than hiding them in a cabinet.

CELEBRATING THE SENSES

Most of us concentrate on the visual aspects of our homes. However, the most enticing environments have something to offer in terms of scent, sound, touch, and taste as well. These often-overlooked sensory cues have tremendous power to evoke a particular time or place. If you have ever stepped into a French *boulangerie,* you may recall the heavenly aroma of fresh-baked bread enveloping you even before you spied the mouthwatering baguettes. A similar experience can be had upon entering French cheese shops and chocolateries.

Of course, you don't want every room to be filled with the aromas of food. Consider topping a nightstand with a bouquet of lavender, tucking thyme-laced sachets in a linen closet, or dressing up a bathroom counter with hand-milled French soaps or potpourri infused with apple, rose, cinnamon, and any other fragrance that conjures images of your favorite sites and seasons.

French background music serves equally well to heighten the mood, whether you are hosting a wine-and-cheese party or enjoying a quiet evening at home. Browse through the international section of local record shops for titles that pique your interest. France prides itself on its regional music, and you will find myriad styles, from Brittany's Celtic fiddle playing and sea chanteys to Parisian café accordion music. Selections also range from quaint folk tunes to nostalgic pop standards by such artists as Edith Piaf and Charles Trenet.

Intriguing textures have long been a staple of provincial decorating—gleaming copper, turned wood, coarse terra-cotta, and rounded fieldstone can all come together to enliven a space with variety. Balance smooth, polished accents with rough, distressed ones to make any room more interesting.

Finally, when it comes to taste, the options are endless. There are arguably more cookbooks devoted to French recipes than to any other nation's cuisine. Try regional specialties, fill a candy dish with tempting French sweets, or browse through gourmet shops for spicy French mustards, aromatic olive oils, and other flavorful flourishes that are sure to add panache to a meal.

OPPOSITE: *The fragrance of lavender emanating from the bouquet on the pillow summons visions of Provence the moment one steps into this charming bedroom tucked under the eaves. Adding to the French country atmosphere are a gauzy canopy, a flock of stenciled birds alighting on the walls, and dainty blue-and-white decorative accents.*

Any number of antiques can find new uses as decorative accents, from vintage birdcages, wire egg baskets, and truffle jars to sets of the round wooden balls used to play *boules* in village squares. The French call such little flea-market gems *brocante.* Not quite junk, not quite valuable, *brocante* is best chosen by assessing its power to intrigue rather than its potential to appreciate in worth.

Another possibility is to obtain French country collectibles from your favorite region—say, wine-making implements from Burgundy, lace-making tools from Normandy, or *santons* from Provence. These little clay "saints" originated after the French Revolution, when public displays of faith were forbidden and sculptors began designing tiny crèche figures for families to display at home. The French developed a fondness for them, and now—in addition to the

LEFT: *A passion for the rich glow of copper inspired this interesting countertop vignette. A tall birdcage, which has found new life as a planter, enhances the display and helps call attention to the copper pieces.*

traditional Nativity pieces—you can find all sorts of petite villagers, from black-smiths to butchers.

Finally, cut flowers provide one of the simplest and most authentic French accents. Not only do they bring the countryside's freshness indoors, they let you underscore colors in your surrounding decor. Plus, they provide an excellent opportunity to play up the spirit of the season—reds and greens at Christmas, oranges and yellows in autumn, and so on.

When it comes to decorative accents, select objects that strike a personal chord with you. These are the pieces that you will cherish for years to come and that will give your home its character.

ABOVE, LEFT: *Marvelously detailed* santons *fill a windowsill with personality.*

ABOVE, RIGHT: *Natural-looking silk roses, such as the ones in this simple tin bucket, can bring a hint of the countryside to your home year-round.*

THE SPORTING LIFE
A PASSION FOR HUNTING AND FISHING

Text by Laurence Sheehan with Carol Sama Sheehan
and Kathryn George · Photographs by William Stites

THE COMPLETE BOOK of HERBS

Franz Marc

PART TWO

ROOM BY ROOM

·⟶W⟵·

♦♦

CHAPTER FIVE

KITCHENS

For centuries, the kitchen has been the heart and soul of the French country home—its source of sustenance, its center of activity. But as anyone who has spent time in France can tell you, what comes *out* in the way of food has always been deemed much more important than what goes *in* in terms of decor. French kitchens are functional, first and foremost. Almost invariably, the arrangement of furnishings and cookware that the visitor finds so irresistible arose naturally, out of practical rather than aesthetic considerations. Chances are that the colorful jumble of ceramic mixing bowls stacked high on a metal baker's rack was not artfully arranged there for show, but simply placed near the counter by a cook who wanted her *batterie de cuisine* (cooking tools) *sous la main* (close at hand). The charmingly battered and timeworn wooden tables, stone sinks, and copper cooking vessels are seldom frivolous accents added for their visual appeal and character. Rather, they have earned their patina through years of everyday use, playing vital roles in the preparation of countless meals.

This unself-conscious, practical beauty is the essence of the French country kitchen's appeal. The unpretentious, durable surfaces; the counters laden with mismatched containers stuffed full of wooden cooking spoons, whisks, and spatulas; the cozy, low-ceilinged milieu; the whisper of history and tradition mingled with the sense of lively energy—all of these elements combine to create a bustling culinary workshop. One glance tells you that this is a warm, welcoming place where

PAGE 78: *Clever trompe l'oeil paintings bring produce-lined shelves and a stash of firewood into this relatively pared-down kitchen.*

BELOW: *Stepping into this kitchen, located in the United States, is like visiting a home in the French countryside, thanks to the Louis XV farm table, the rush-seat ladder-back chairs, and the antique buffet à deux corps. An old-fashioned butcher block provides an abundance of counter space, which in typical fashion, has been filled with bread baskets, cookware, and other kitchen implements.*

OPPOSITE: *Exposed wooden ceiling beams, hanging bouquets of dried flowers, and a beautiful collection of faïence fill this French country–style kitchen with a heartwarming sense of nostalgia.*

the air is often charged with anticipation and laced with rich, savory cooking aromas—the promise of delicious cassoulets, soufflés, terrines, and tarts to come.

THE BASIC INGREDIENTS

While French country living rooms, dining rooms, and bedrooms convey a sense of soft, almost luxurious comfort, kitchens tend to retain a more overtly rustic demeanor. Weathered wooden trestle tables are preferred over sleek glass or lacquered designs, and rush-seat ladder-back chairs are favored over cushy, upholstered ones. Far from stark or dreary, these furnishings give a room an appealing, farm-fresh simplicity. Tables often play host to flowers, colorful dishes, and bowls of ripe fruit, and chairs sometimes sport an uplifting shade of paint topped off by a bold flourish. A brick red chair, for example, might boast slats painted canary yellow, while a forest green one might feature stalks of painted pink flowers winding up its legs for a whimsical touch.

Signs of history are apt to be more prevalent in the kitchen than in other rooms. After all, in homes that date back a century or more, the kitchen is usually the oldest part of the structure—the original communal chamber where family members would cook, eat, sleep, and relax. Two time-honored hallmarks of this important space are exposed wooden ceiling beams and a gargantuan hearth. While the latter is seldom used for cooking as it was in ages past, it continues to garner attention by offering a crackling fire or showcasing an intriguing display—a grouping of ceramic jugs filled with enormous sprays of dried flowers, for instance. Above the mantel, an antique hoe, a vintage pitchfork, or some other old-fashioned farm tool might find new life as a decorative accent.

Natural materials and coarse, irregular textures dominate the architecture. Stone or terra-cotta tile tends to be the flooring of choice, providing an underlying sense of rugged, natural beauty. For walls, painted or whitewashed stucco prevails, sometimes accented with exposed wooden cross beams. Old, weathered doors, many of which still boast their original ironwork, are treasured for their abundant character. Every element seems designed to endure centuries of heavy use—and indeed, many already have. Those features that have stood the test of time not only offer a connection to the past but also lend provincial kitchens a hearty, primitive flavor, as robust as French country cooking itself.

Happily, it's quite easy to capture the same look in your own kitchen. Start by emphasizing warm colors, such as rosy browns and soft, buttery yellows;

these tones not only recall the interiors of rural France but also provide a flattering backdrop for wood furnishings—another ingredient for a French country–style kitchen. You could also incorporate reclaimed antique tile, field-stone, or brick for walls or floors. (If your kitchen is small, note that larger floor tiles suggest a bigger space, especially when laid on the diagonal to pull your eye to the far end of the room.) Other options would be to find wallpaper that resembles distressed brick or tile or to hire an artist to simulate the look with a trompe l'oeil design.

Indeed, incorporating clever wall-painting techniques is a favorite way to add a dash of whimsy to a kitchen. A pantry in rural France might be overgrown

with fanciful stenciled grapevines or accented with French words of culinary wisdom that wrap around its perimeter like a chair rail. Trompe l'oeil barnyards, hillsides, and sunflower fields will not only evoke another world but create a feeling of depth—an illusion that is especially desirable in small spaces.

Tile provides another popular decorative accent. It can be used sparingly—say, to line a backsplash or stove hood—or lavishly, covering entire counters and walls. Long-lasting, hard-wearing, and easy to clean, tile offers many practical benefits along with its virtually unlimited potential for imaginative applications. A quartet of lovely antique ceramic tiles adorned with red-and-white roosters could be centered on a wall behind a stove and surrounded with solid black

ABOVE, LEFT: *Charming depictions of chickens and eggs turn ordinary cabinets and drawers into works of art.*

ABOVE, RIGHT: *This eye-catching alcove celebrates an oenophile's passion, with names of wines hand-painted on tiles lining the edge of the counter. Continuing the theme is the French phrase for "wine cellar" on the backsplash.*

OPPOSITE: *Knotty pine cabinetry and terra-cotta flooring lend a hint of old-style rural charm to this kitchen, offsetting the updated stainless steel range and hood. A plate rack recalls the traditional* vaisselier *while honoring the provincial tradition of keeping necessities at the ready. Note the French canisters tucked behind the fresh apple pie on the counter.*

or red tiles to create a striking medallion. Or, for a more subtle effect, a counter could be covered in simple white tiles and brightened by a few specialty tiles—perhaps painted with green ivy leaves—here and there. This accent color could be played up by hanging a green-and-white toile swag at the window above the sink.

When it comes to appliances, the French favor function over fashion. Gas stoves are de rigueur—as they are in most chefs' kitchens—prized for the quick, controllable heat they produce. Refrigerators, sinks, and other items vary widely, based on such factors as available space and personal preference. If a fifty-year-old icebox still performs well, chances are its owner won't even think about replacing it. On the other hand, a sleek, brushed-chrome refrigerator would not look out of place in a provincial home. In keeping with the eclectic nature of French country decor, venerable antiques often sit cheek by jowl with state-of-the-art newcomers, managing to blend remarkably well. A high-tech dishwasher might rub shoulders with a vintage cast-iron range, while an antique bread box could share counter space with a microwave oven and a deluxe food processor. Let practical considerations such as cost and convenience guide your appliance-buying decisions; then conjure up a French country atmosphere with the surrounding elements.

CHARMING CLUTTER

The quintessential French country kitchen is hardly a minimalist's cup of tea. A group of copper saucepans is likely to dangle from a decorative pot rack, along with strands of garlic, dried herbs, and woven baskets. Below, counters are probably lined with a cornucopia of cooking wines, olive oils, marmalade jars, and wooden bowls filled with lemons, tomatoes, and other fresh produce. Even the tidiest of provincial kitchens is apt to have an assortment of its owner's best-loved linens and cooking tools situated out in the open, where they are within easy reach. Improvisation rules, and clever new spots can always be found to stash much-used items. This busy, almost cluttered look is actually an essential part of the style's relaxed, informal allure.

Open shelving, either built-in or freestanding, is almost always found in one corner or another. One of the most common forms is the metal baker's rack, which usually features decoratively curved edging. Often stacked with colorful tea towels and dishes, it is designed to let air circulate beneath it, making it a perfect place to let hot dishes cool and damp ones dry. Old wooden *vaisseliers*—either left natural to showcase their wood grain or painted cheerful colors like celery green and creamy blue—are another favorite when it comes to storing items in the open. Occasionally, the backs of the shelves are covered with printed

paper to enhance the display of a particular china pattern. One of the simplest ways to keep your decor interesting is to change the dishes in the *vaisselier*—perhaps crisp whiteware for spring and chunky mustard-yellow pottery for autumn. You could also line the shelves with a mixture of pieces from several sets of china in complementary patterns.

Copper is the "gold standard" for cookware in France, beloved for its unparalleled ability to heat quickly and evenly and to bring whipped egg whites to a light, frothy consistency. (The latter quality makes it a necessity in Brittany, a region famed for its delicious, light-as-air crepes.) If you already own cookware and don't want to invest in pricey copper pans, you might purchase a set of affordable copperplate canisters to brighten a counter, place a shiny copperplate teapot on the stove when it is not in use, hang a pair of chocolate molds in the shapes of ladybugs and bees on a wall, or add any number of other affordable copperplate touches, from planters to overhead light fixtures.

RIGHT: *A one-of-a-kind antique becomes an impressive focal point when used as the base of a kitchen island. Thanks to the space's understated neutral backdrop, the eye is drawn instantly to the unusual treasure from yesteryear. The room offers a good example of how a single distinctive item can inject an abundance of nostalgic French flavor into an otherwise modern space.*

WINE CELLARS

ABOVE: *A former linen closet was transformed into a sophisticated wine cellar with walls of vivid blue enhanced by a motif of meandering grapevines. A petite bistro table and a pair of blue-painted chairs form an intimate tasting area, while French vintners' accoutrements offer intriguing decorative accents.*

Given the French people's longtime love affair with wine, it's no surprise that any self-respecting country home has a generous supply on hand. In many a dwelling, favorite vintages are stored on a capacious rack in a corner of the kitchen. But in other homes, such as grand old country manors, wines may be kept in a wine cellar—a cavernous underground chamber, full of atmosphere and dusty bottles of lush, full-bodied merlots and delicate, dry chablis. If you, too, are an oenophile, you might bring a bit of old France home by closing off one end of a refinished basement or refurbishing an extra closet near the kitchen to create a wine cellar.

When it comes to storing the wine, interior designer Carole Winer, owner and founder of Country Loft Antiques in Woodbury, Connecticut, favors certain modular terra-cotta brick holders in wooden frames. "They're designed by a 150-year-old French manufacturer, so they have an authentically old French flavor," she says. On a decorative note, Winer often calls upon old basketry from French vineyards to adorn wine cellar walls.

Indeed, there are numerous possibilities for enhancing a wine cellar with eye-catching accents. While the bottles themselves create instant ambience, why not enliven the setting with a few decorative touches that will conjure up the spirit of a French vineyard? One clever idea is to panel the walls with the sides of wooden wine boxes, each branded with a different French vintner's imprint. You could also create an artful display by framing a collection of colorful wine labels. Another alternative is to brighten walls with posters of vintage French wine advertisements.

If you're fond of antiques, you might also search for old-fashioned vintners' tools to use ornamentally. The more rusted and weather-beaten they are, the more character they will exude when displayed on a wall or simply propped in a corner as decorative *objets*. Some wine lovers even develop a passion for unusual corkscrews or tasting implements and use them to line a shelf, where they make intriguing conversation pieces. Add a small collapsible wine-tasting table if you have room, and voilà—a cellar worthy of the finest French vintages.

Although used more sparingly than in other rooms, fabric, too, finds a home in the kitchen. Cheerful Provençal prints and gingham checks are popular not just for table linens but for tea towels, aprons, oven mitts, and valances as well. Affordable and easy to store, Provençal fabrics provide one of the simplest ways to give your kitchen a pinch of French country seasoning. What's more, because the colors and patterns of Provençal prints tend to mix and match effortlessly, you can easily add new ones and take out others to achieve a quick change of scenery. This revolving decor can receive its cues from the seasons or simply your own personal whims.

Perhaps the best part of the French country kitchen is its tendency to boast imaginative accents. Anything can add character, from a vintage cast-iron doorstop in the shape of a plump, jovial pig (farm animals, vegetables, and fruits are popular motifs) to a timeworn nineteenth-century wall clock, its paint flaking and its hands lost long ago. Even items that might not seem traditionally appropriate for a kitchen—botanical prints and framed oil paintings of ships, for instance—can find their way in among the pots and pans and seem perfectly at ease.

Let your creative juices guide you as you decorate. The more personalized the accents you include, the more homey and lived-in your kitchen will feel. A set of canisters bearing the French words for such staples as sugar (*sucre*), flour (*farine*), and coffee (*café*) can make a striking statement when clustered on a shelf or counter. A vintage wire egg basket placed under a framed print of hens can become a witty vignette. The best way to honor the authentic spirit of French country is to leave whatever you use and treasure most out in plain view, whether it happens to be a rack of fine wines brought home from last year's vacation in Saint-Étienne or a humble collection of well-thumbed and battered cookbooks.

ABOVE: *Sporting a sunny shade of yellow, vintage canisters designed to hold culinary staples form a cheerful still life.*

❧❧

CHAPTER SIX

LIVING ROOMS AND DINING ROOMS

So renowned is the French flair for conversation that the word *salon* (the French equivalent of "living room") has become synonymous with erudite cultural gatherings. History's most celebrated salons, of course, were in Paris, but the love of scintillating, articulate discussion is just as abundant in the countryside. Though hardly known for gregariousness toward strangers, the French pride themselves on being gracious hosts and tend to entertain often—doing so with a style all their own. Dining and living rooms set the stage for lively evenings with friends and family, providing environments where one can linger happily for hours enjoying the warm glow of candlelight, ample glasses of mellow merlot, mouthwatering cassoulets, creamy Camembert, and spirited chats about theater, art, literature, travel, philosophy, and of course, the joys of life in the French countryside.

Sally McConnell and her husband, Bringier—founders of the French Country Living shop and catalog—fell under the spell of this warm, convivial lifestyle when they moved to Paris in the 1980s. "Friends would invite us to their country homes for the weekend, and we would be embraced by this sort of joie de vivre," she recalls. "It seemed so comfortable, so colorful and relaxed and confident." She notes that her American customers seem to crave this "celebration of life and home."

Perhaps the most alluring quality of French country living and dining rooms is that, though they exude elegance and beauty, they are nonetheless welcoming

and approachable. Full of vibrant colors and energetic patterns, they set the stage for animated conversation and laughter. Formal and informal styles merge into a sort of robust sophistication that brims with personality but is never pretentious. An elegantly curved French Regency chair will be offset by a casual Provençal print–covered pillow nestled in the crook of its arm, and a lavishly gilded mirror will be counterbalanced by a humble rush-seat bench positioned beneath it. Nothing is so refined that it intimidates. In much the same way that an exquisitely carved eighteenth-century *buffet à deux corps* was crafted to play an important role in daily life rather than to be appreciated from a distance, French country interiors are designed to be lived in and heartily enjoyed. As the French have understood for years, the more fully you use your home, the greater pleasure you will derive from it.

ROOMS FOR LIVING

It wasn't until the eighteenth century that the salon came into vogue among the French aristocracy and replaced the bedroom as the fashionable place to greet and entertain visitors. Since appearances were of the utmost importance, the nobility lavished more care on the salon than on any other room in the house. This prominent space was appointed with the finest furnishings and draped in the most sumptuous fabrics. Great pains were taken to ensure that every detail expressed a sense of status and style.

Another century elapsed before the salon became an essential part of the home for the common folk. When it did, the new room was usually fashioned from what had once been either the dwelling's sole communal chamber or an adjacent stable. Hence, many provincial living rooms boast a wealth of rural architectural details, still visible despite the various modernizations that may have occurred over the years. Enormous old brick-and-stone hearths offer striking reminders of a bygone age when families would cook over the open fire. Ancient rough-hewn beams watch over luxurious damask curtains, and worn flagstone floors peek out beneath Aubusson carpets or elegant Louis XV–style settees. All of these time-honored structural features serve as testaments to a house's humble roots. In fact, this juxtaposition of elegance and rusticity is a basic component of French country style.

Most homeowners in rural France celebrate wear and tear in their architectural details. A former stable wall displaying the scars of time is less likely to be

PAGE 92: *A crackling blaze in an elegant fireplace contributes to the convivial spirit of this gathering area. French country decorating often takes a less rustic approach to outfitting the living room than to furnishing the kitchen, a point evidenced here by the generous use of upholstery and carpeting. The rich red tones of the painting echo the colors in the sofa, while the modern, abstract style presents a pleasing juxtaposition with the venerable hearth and the traditional architectural details of the room.*

OPPOSITE: *Vivid hues and patterns blend easily in this living area, which includes a boldly striped sofa, an Oriental rug, and a pair of armchairs covered in a Provençal print. Throw pillows in a similar shade of blue accent the red sofa, while ones with hints of red rest on the blue chairs to unite the furnishings. By arranging a cozy conversation area in the center of a large room, the owners have achieved a sense of intimacy and definition. However, the sitting area still feels connected to the adjacent dining space, thanks to the blue-and-red print cushions on the ladder-back chairs and the use of similar woods in both zones.*

replastered than to receive a fresh coat of paint that accentuates its rich character. Similarly, a weathered, soot-blackened wooden mantel is apt to be transformed into an intriguing focal point lined with dried flowers rather than be replaced or downplayed. (The embracing of this timeworn look is not limited to architectural features, but applies to wood furnishings as well.)

Whether you plan to decorate an entire living room or simply add a splash of French country style to the decor you already have, the four cornerstones of floor, ceiling, walls, and windows make a fine starting point. It's possible to transform even the most modern-looking space, full of right angles and fresh plaster, into a fairy-tale setting by bringing in reclaimed timbering for the ceiling

OPPOSITE: *A grand fireplace, nearly large enough to stand in, harks back to the days before central heating—when the family gathered round a roaring hearth on cold winter evenings. The sunny yellow wash on the walls adds to the warmth of the setting, while white-painted ceiling beams counterbalance the heaviness of the hearth and the paneled door.*

LEFT: *In lieu of a mantel, the fireplace boasts a painted panel featuring a still life of fruit and flowers. The tile flooring in front of the hearth blends in with the room's many reddish-brown tones.*

and nineteenth-century flagstones for the floor. However, you don't need to go to such lengths to capture the spirit of French country romance. Instead of introducing new materials, you can work with the framework that you already have. Walls provide a wonderful canvas, and something as basic as the right paint treatment will have a big impact. In Provence, vivid colors take a room from dull to dramatic with one coat of paint. Favorite shades, drawn from the beautiful natural landscape, include deep vermilion, bittersweet orange, ocher, and olive green.

Equally popular means of establishing a lively French country backdrop include patterned wallpaper, colorful fabrics stretched across entire walls, faux

RIGHT: *Ornate trompe l'oeil portrait frames make a bewitching statement, especially when juxtaposed against such rugged elements as weathered wood trim and a scuffed floor. These features merge with an array of strongly sculptural objects on the table to lend the scene the bohemian flavor of an artist's atelier.*

wood paneling, decorative molding, texturing, and even trompe l'oeil. A series of cleverly painted ivory-and-ebony trompe l'oeil portraits—suspended from gracefully painted ribbons—might "hang" on a wall, for example. (A touch like this is bound to make visitors look twice.) You could enhance such a color scheme with grand, floor-length curtains in black-and-cream-striped taffeta, accented with black-and-gold fringe and tasseled tiebacks. If a more rustic look is to your liking, turn to rag rolling to simulate the uneven look of coarse stucco that is characteristic of nineteenth-century French farmhouses. Reinforce this earthy appeal with a few rough-hewn wooden furnishings, a generous basket of firewood or pinecones placed near the hearth, and a bowl of apple-scented pot-pourri. For a touch of country-manor grandeur, incorporate cross panes for the windows and introduce a trompe l'oeil reproduction of one of the magnificent Aubusson tapestries that graced fashionable châteaux in the eighteenth century. Stone angels rescued from a country chapel could make an appropriate flourish for a nearby mantel.

When you are satisfied with the backdrop of your room, turn your attention toward the furnishings. Traditionally, prized possessions were situated in the living room for visitors to admire—a grandfather clock if the family owned one, graceful armchairs or a lovely settee, perhaps even a small carved cabinet on which a few examples of fine porcelain and other treasures would be placed.

The approach is still employed in today's French living rooms, where cherished antiques share space with new acquisitions, all prominently positioned to be appreciated and enjoyed by guests as well as owners. Although an heirloom armoire—its cornice practically brushing the ceiling—might be generations older and heads taller than the other living room furnishings, such characteristics would not necessarily prevent it from taking up residence in the midst of the gathering area. Indeed, both scale and period are often ignored to charming effect, giving French country living rooms an appealing eclectic flavor and an aura of timeless chic.

Such qualities are enhanced by the French tendency to acquire and collect furnishings gradually over time rather than to purchase them as a set, and to honor history-laden heirlooms rather than relegate them to some out-of-the-way spot in favor of trendy home accessories. As a result, nothing matches perfectly,

LEFT: *Black-and-white toile-covered furnishings with crimson piping give this room a sophisticated edge. Toile is often paired with more tailored patterns, like the checks shown here, to curb its somewhat fussy look.*

ABOVE: *A lamp boasting a pretty floral shade and a black-and-gold tole base blends amicably with red-and-white floral curtains nearby. Cherished antiques, including a Victorian folding fan, a handful of leather-bound volumes, and a small marble statue, fill the vignette with sentimental appeal.*

SMALL SPACES, DRAMATIC STATEMENTS

Though often overlooked when it comes to decorating, foyers, staircase landings, and hallways can prove ideal spots for a French country flourish. While residents and guests do not tend to spend long, concentrated amounts of time in these areas, as they do in living and dining rooms, such transition spaces do receive a lot of traffic as people come and go. As a result, there are lots of opportunities for objects on display to be admired.

In compact spaces, it is best to limit decorative accessories to just a few well-chosen pieces. Doing so will prevent such areas from feeling cluttered or cramped. Fortunately, it takes only a couple of accents to fill a foyer or hallway with French country charm.

As you contemplate these types of spaces—especially an entryway—consider both decorative and practical features. Taking both aesthetics and functionality into account will make your transition areas more hospitable. In a foyer, you could make a powerful design statement by placing a ceramic vase glazed in Provence's trademark celadon and mustard tones atop a diminutive wooden table. Fill the container with sunny yellow flowers to give guests a cheerful greeting. For a practical yet equally attractive touch, add a coordinating shallow dish in which keys can be kept handy. And don't overlook the area beneath the table, which can play host to a vintage leather valise or a wicker basket without compromising the flow of traffic. (The basket can double as a place to store scarves and gloves.) If you have the space, instead of a table you could situate a small writing desk in the entry. Such a piece will create a homey, lived-in feel and provide a convenient spot for stashing mail.

Another bonus of entryways and the like is that they are wonderful places in which to experiment with unusual decorative techniques that you might not want to try in a larger space—say, a coat of bold terra-cotta paint, some brightly

ABOVE: *A distressed cobalt blue paint treatment imbues this foyer with a sense of drama while providing a flattering backdrop for a cherry console table. The antique-looking piece was inspired by an eighteenth-century French writing desk.*

striped wallpaper, or even a trompe l'oeil effect. You could cover one wall of a mudroom, for instance, with a whimsical mural of a French vineyard, complete with scenes of peasants harvesting grapes in the distance. Such a strategy will add panache to an otherwise dull room and, if executed well, visually enlarge the small space. (Keep in mind that color schemes should harmonize with any adjacent rooms that are clearly visible from the area in question.)

If your landing or hallway is too narrow for a table, bench, or bookcase, you might consider building a decorative niche into a wall and using it to display antique Limoges porcelain, *santons*, or any other decorative objects. This approach not only introduces a striking architectural feature but also provides a stable, recessed, out-of-the-way spot where fragile treasures are less likely to be knocked over and broken—a decided advantage in homes with children and pets.

yet everything harmonizes beautifully, blended subtly through color, pattern, wood grain, or simply the fact that each piece has sentimental significance for its owner. To achieve such a happy mélange in your own living area, you need to possess a certain level of confidence and have faith in your own tastes. Embarking upon such an endeavor might sound intimidating if you've never tried it, but it is actually a brilliantly easy way to have fun decorating and to make your home less generic and more enjoyable.

When buying and arranging furnishings, usability should rival aesthetics on your priority list. Decide which items are likely to serve your needs and which will tempt you to spend the most time in your living room. If you have children or pets, create an environment that is beautiful *and* family-friendly. Eschew easily scratched, smooth wood finishes in favor of distressed or unpolished surfaces, and choose dark colors or vivacious patterns rather than whites, pale pastels, and

ABOVE: *A cornucopia of patterns and colors gives this room its personality. Stripes, toiles, plaids, and solids in mouthwatering fruit tints mingle harmoniously on a harlequin-patterned rug. An intricately painted armoire that nearly grazes the ceiling offers the casual space a hint of grandiloquence.*

solids, which show stains easily. Instead of reupholstering seating or investing in new chairs and couches, consider slipcovers, which can be removed for cleaning or changed for a fresh look.

As you flip through magazines and catalogs, tear out photographs of French country furnishings that speak to your aesthetic sensibility. Then lay these images out on a table, play around with different groupings, and determine which elements work well together. Be sure to take into account which furnishings and accents best meet your practical needs, too. If you adore an item that is beyond your price range, search local furniture stores, other catalogs, or even flea markets for an affordable alternative. You might also ask a knowledgeable retailer for advice regarding how to find a less expensive reproduction or how to achieve a similar effect. Often there are creative, less costly ways to replicate the look you hope to obtain. For example, if you love the appearance of antique painted tables but don't want to invest in them, you might find a pair of pretty painted wooden trays large enough to cover the tops of your end tables.

Not surprisingly, warm colors are favorites for living room upholstery and curtains, and great joy is taken in mixing vibrant hues, patterns, and textures to heighten visual interest. Fabrics also provide one of the quickest, most practical ways to spruce up the existing decor of a room. If you adore an armchair's

RIGHT: *An enticing assortment of blue, yellow, and white cotton prints gives this stylish living room a lighthearted spirit almost reminiscent of chinoiserie, which tends to feature meandering patterns and blue-and-white color schemes. Though a number of pieces in the space are quite impressive in scale—particularly the Louis XVI–style ottoman—clustering furnishings around the fireplace engenders a sense of intimacy that is undeniably conducive to conversation.*

silhouette but have tired of its pale peach tone, you might freshen up the piece by adding a boisterous toss pillow bearing an orange floral mini-print and hints of peach or by draping a pretty peach, orange, pale blue, and turquoise plaid afghan over it. Those with a penchant for Parisian refinement might balance the formality of jacquard couches and curtains with a smattering of homier touches, including oil paintings in tarnished gilt frames and reproduction furnishings boasting deliberately faded upholstery or crackled paint finishes to suggest an aged look.

To help establish the convivial mood of a French salon, call upon the soft, diffused lighting of candles and small reading lamps. You could also create enchanting sconces by placing low-wattage bulbs behind semitransparent, woven olive oil filters (*scourtins*). Mirrors will also increase the amount of reflective warmth. Next, arrange inviting vignettes. A snug-feeling sitting area can be achieved by drawing a pair of armchairs close to the fireplace—a perfect spot for a chat à deux. To create a conversation area that can accommodate a larger gathering but still feel cozy, a close arrangement of sofas and chairs around a low coffee table will do the trick; place an Oriental rug beneath the coffee table to add warmth and help anchor the sitting area in the midst of the larger space. In the end, you'll have a feeling of intimacy that defies the physical size of the room.

Finally, personalized collections and expressive accents provide the special touches needed to give life to a living room. If you love books, line every shelf with them and stack attractive hardbacks on the coffee table. If you adore photographs or artwork, why restrict yourself to one picture per wall? The French often cover a large area over a couch with an attention-grabbing collection of images in a variety of frames. Make the most of the different surfaces in the space. A writing desk might provide the ideal spot for a collection of chinoiserie or tole boxes, and a windowsill might offer a resting place for a trio of Lyons' beloved nineteenth-century puppets—Guignol and his fellow stock characters, inspired by Italian commedia dell'arte. Another option is to honor a favorite region. If you have a special place in your heart for Brittany, line your mantel with wooden buoys and other nautical elements from this area. If your dreams take you to the south of France, perch a pair of ceramic cicadas—classic symbols of Provence—next to a couch, where they can peer up at visitors. You might even extend the theme to the windows by selecting curtains embellished with a print of tiny gold cicadas on a wheat or buttercup background.

LEFT: *A diminutive writing desk and artwork positioned low on the walls help draw the eye downward, reducing the imposing dimensions of the room and easing the formality of the manor house's architecture.*

GRACIOUS DINING

Since France is one of the world's gastronomic capitals, where people are passionate about favorite wines and fiercely loyal to regional cheeses, it is hardly surprising that cuisine—rather than decor—plays the starring role in the *salle à manger* (dining room). This space's primary function is to create an inviting environment in which to savor delicious meals. Toward that end, most of the decorative attention is focused on the table. Invigorating colors and jaunty patterns are layered and combined in countless ways to set the stage for savory

BELOW: *Sunny yellow chargers, blue-and-white china, and Provençal-print napkins lay the groundwork for a festive gathering. Cut-crystal goblets, brass candlesticks, and a luxuriant centerpiece of roses provide elegant finishing touches.*

soups, scrumptious main courses, and delectable desserts. This is not to say, however, that the other elements of the room can be ignored. Walls, windows, and furnishings all play important supporting roles.

Before you begin decorating your dining room, take into consideration the time of day in which you will use it the most. If you adore leisurely Sunday brunches but seldom prepare elaborate dinners, think about painting the walls in one of the lighter shades representative of French country style—perhaps nutmeg or toasted almond. While dark tones create a theatrical backdrop for evening repasts, they can appear drab on sunny afternoons. That said, if you favor romantic candlelight dinners, opt for a deep shade such as amber or

RIGHT: *Mustard walls and a celadon-painted cupboard create a welcoming backdrop for meals. Informality and sophistication come together through the use of rush-seat ladder-back chairs dressed up with decorative flourishes, and casual checked curtains made more opulent with tasseled tiebacks.*

russet—equally evocative of French country interiors—since pale tones have a tendency to look faded and lackluster once the sun goes down.

Light or dark, dining room walls in French country homes are usually covered in warm, welcoming tones. Among the favorites are rose and crimson, apricot and fiery orange, and buttery yellow and luminous gold—colors that quicken the pulse and sharpen the appetite. Curtains echo the palette of the walls and tend to cascade down to the floor. Trimmed in fringe and braiding, they are often quite sumptuous. Popular fabrics and designs range from floral-patterned damasks and plaid taffetas to flamboyant cotton toiles and spirited checks.

Because the dining room is usually adjacent to the living area, care is given to creating a smooth transition between the two. Colors and patterns needn't match precisely, but they should coexist peacefully rather than create a jarring effect. It's interesting to note that since the dining room is a more recent addition to the French country home, it tends to lack the living room's striking old architectural details, though often it boasts larger, more abundant windows.

When it comes to selecting furnishings, the best place to start is the table. After all, this piece will be at the center of your mealtime gatherings. Before you embark upon your quest for a table, ask yourself a few practical questions. How many people will eat in the room on a regular basis? How often do you have

ABOVE, LEFT: *Neighboring rooms with sight lines that run directly from one to the next work best when their color palettes harmonize. Here, a living room is awash in gloriously vibrant shades of tangerine and gold, as is the dining room beyond the doorway. Unpretentious country touches such as Provençal-print curtains, a pair of santons perched on the mantel, and a clay pot brimming with sunflowers seem quite at home amid the formality of a damask sofa and a chandelier twinkling with crystal bobeches.*

ABOVE, RIGHT: *Stepping through the doorway, one enters a dining room brimming with the same exuberant hues that energize the living room. The wood furnishings set a distinctly less formal mood than that of the living room yet maintain the cordial ambience established by the sun-kissed palette.*

guests over for meals, and how many do you usually invite? How many diners can the room hold comfortably?

Use your answers to help you find the table that will best suit your lifestyle. If you love to host dinner parties but have limited space, an expandable model with removable leaves that can easily be stowed under a sideboard might provide a practical solution. (You may also be able to find attractive folding chairs that can be tucked away in a closet when not in use.) If you would like the room to serve as the setting for quiet dinners with your immediate family, avoid a grandiose table that you'll be uncomfortable using on a daily basis.

Other furnishings that usually take up residence in the dining room include a buffet, a sideboard, a *buffet à deux corps,* or perhaps a towering *vaisselier.* Depending on the level of formality you seek, you might choose cheerfully painted flea-market finds or gleaming mahogany antiques. Paintings, prints, decorative plates, or a pretty clock may adorn the walls, and a few choice collectibles may grace a neighboring shelf, but by and large, decorative accents are more understated in the dining room than in other parts of the French country home. The restraint is deliberate to avoid an overly busy environment that might detract from or overpower the food being served.

Fortunately, you needn't be a gourmet chef—in fact, you needn't cook at all—to discover the delights of setting a beautiful table in the French country style. Dishes, linens, and other decorative accents come together in a festive display of color and pattern. As with other elements of French country decor, though the individual components do not necessarily match, they demonstrate a powerful sense of unity.

When it comes to table linens, French country style embraces all sorts of arrangements—including the use of place mats sans tablecloth. However, the classic French treatment entails a layering process. Typically, one long cloth, which cascades to the floor, is topped by a shorter cloth in a complementary color or pattern. This second—usually lighter-toned—textile drapes over the table, with its edges stretching toward the ground but revealing plenty of the underlying fabric. (A protective cloth may also be hidden under both layers.) As is the case with upholstery and window treatments, toiles happily pair with checks and stripes, and plaids mix with florals. Similarly, Provençal prints bearing different motifs or the same motifs in harmonizing color schemes also join together to wish diners bon appétit.

Napkins make an important decorative contribution as well. These highly serviceable accessories not only attend to guests' needs but also help to dress up

OPPOSITE: *A venerable oval table with turned-wood legs is flanked by plush wing chairs in this hospitable room, which can do double duty as both salon and* salle à manger. *The charmingly mismatched seating conjures a snug, comfortable milieu where one feels free to while away an evening engrossed in a good book or conversation, or indulge in a rejuvenating nap—like the dog nestled against the chair arm. Enhancing the room's cozy allure are the crimson-shaded brass lamp, the distinguished carved armoire, and the heavy drapes guarding against winter chills.*

RIGHT: *A cotton toile tablecloth lays the groundwork for a lively table, dressed up with matching napkins as well as plates in coordinating hues. Placing solid red dishes beneath toile-inspired china not only makes the latter stand out but also spices up the setting.*

the table. Cornflower blue and creamy peach plaid, for instance, could be used to bring out the amber and teal in a floral chintz tablecloth. Or poppy-colored napkins with a vertically swirling vine design could be introduced to play up the red tones of a multihued, striped place mat. Because napkins are relatively inexpensive, they provide a convenient means for altering the look of your table when you want a change of scenery or mood.

In fact, table linens in general have an enormous impact on a dining area's ambience. To conjure up a sunny morning in the south of France, you might cover a table with a Provençal cloth featuring such colors as sapphire, cerulean, and white, and then top it off with a chunky earthenware pitcher of lavender. For an intimate dinner later that evening, you could simply replace the above-mentioned elements with a burgundy damask tablecloth, elegant silver candlesticks, and a silver bowl of red roses, creating a setting romantic enough to rival a country château.

Variety comes into play not only with table linens but with dishware, too. Unlike the traditional American table, where every dish tends to be carefully matched, improvisation and imagination dominate the scene. In all but the most formal of meals, colors and patterns are deftly mixed. Berry red bowls might accent crisp blue-and-white chinoiserie dishes, for example, or serving pieces

ABOVE: *Jewels for the table: sapphire blue vases bearing sprays of fresh flowers in the same buttery hue as the place mats make a winsome centerpiece for a casual table. The yellow-and-blue color combination has long been popular in the French provinces.*

LEFT: *Morning coffee awaits an early riser on a sun-drenched table. Far from restrained, French country style embraces riotous explosions of color and pattern, as this blooming garden of indigo and saffron backed by dainty lace curtains suggests.*

RIGHT: *Provençal prints, like this upbeat* indienne *tablecloth dotted with sunflowers, are favorites in rural dining rooms. The chunky blue and mustard-colored earthenware dishes pair effortlessly with the vivacious linens.*

embellished with sunflowers might inject a note of vitality alongside cobalt blue dinner plates.

For authentic country flavor, many Francophiles turn to faïence. This hand-painted white earthenware—bedecked with charmingly naive depictions of flowers, animals, and French peasants—was inspired by a similar type of Italian pottery made during the Middle Ages in the town of Faenza (from which it receives its name). One of the best-loved types of faïence is Quimper, which comes from Brittany and features a motif of Breton peasants in traditional dress, the man with a walking stick and the woman with an apron and bonnet. The factory has been handcrafting these wonderful primitive-style designs since 1690. "What most people find appealing is the fact that, because each piece is handmade by half a dozen artists from casting to glazing to painting, no two are exactly alike," says Heather Card, general manager of Quimper Faïence retail stores in the United States. "And of course, there's the heritage. More Americans are beginning to discover Quimper, and they love the idea that the factory has been around for more than three centuries." Although faïence has traditionally been associated with casual meals, Card notes that it looks quite at home on more sophisticated tables, too, and can easily be dressed up with linen napkins and crystal goblets.

Perhaps the best-known formal china from France is Limoges. Contrary to popular belief, Limoges is not a brand but the name of the town in which this type of porcelain originated.

During the 1600s, when delicate blue-and-white china plates first began arriving in Europe in the holds of merchant ships from China, they caused an enormous sensation. Europeans adored them and spent the next century attempting to replicate the creamy, durable porcelain. When large deposits of white kaolin clay—the key ingredient in porcelain—were discovered near Limoges in the mid-1700s, they were able to accomplish this goal. Soon the new material began to supplant faïence as the tableware of choice, and Limoges' fame spread. Two centuries later, the city is still a center for fine china (one of the best-known manufacturers is Haviland, founded in the 1840s); gorgeous designs run the gamut from delicate pastel flowers and shells to bold geometric motifs in primary colors.

LEFT: *A quaint table in a Brittany cottage boasts a handsome lace tablecloth and an assortment of faïence. Both crafts were historical specialties of the region.*

Baccarat lead crystal, another exquisite French export, makes an elegant accent, as do antique silver accessories, flickering candles, romantic chandeliers, and imaginative centerpieces. Instead of having a flower arrangement as the focal point, a table might boast a lovely crystal bowl piled high with sugared fruit or a gold platter laden with pomegranates, pinecones, and rosy red Seckel pears. Even a pretty basket of flour-dusted loaves of bread surrounded by bowls of shiny black and green olives can make a beautiful table decoration atop a Provençal cloth. For a rustic twist, use a woven basket full of apples, a cluster of interestingly shaped candles, or even a bowl of floating candles and blossoms ringed by pretty shells. (This last approach is especially fitting for an evening meal in the garden.)

Like an artist's canvas, the table provides endless opportunities for imaginative creations. Let the meal you are serving, the time of day, and the nature of the occasion inspire you. To enhance a formal Thanksgiving dinner, you could combine similar yet distinct sets of elegant French porcelain; ivory dinner plates with chocolate brown edging might pair well with gold-rimmed ivory bread plates, for example. By contrast, a hearty winter stew might call for the folk-art appeal of faïence. If you already own a set of china, you might collect interesting accent pieces to mix with it. Even basic white dishes flanked by blue goblets, whimsical yellow-and-blue egg cups, and vintage silver will transport breakfast guests to the French countryside.

Indeed, an unassuming set of white or ivory china can provide the foundation for a wide variety of striking tablescapes. If you're hosting an elegant winter affair, jazz these simple plates up by placing lustrous gold chargers beneath them. Then heighten the feeling of luxury by positioning a ruby red wineglass beside each dish. For a summer gathering, the same set of china can take on an entirely different mood. Lay the groundwork with an airy blue-and-white-checked tablecloth placed atop a solid red one. Add the white dishes to the scene, and top them off with cut-glass salad bowls, alternating between red and blue at every place setting. In the end, you'll have the perfect stage for celebrating both Bastille Day and Independence Day!

Of course, no element will make a more favorable impression on a provincial table than delicious French food. Why not peruse one of the countless French regional cookbooks available and experiment with a few simple recipes for omelettes or salads? If you prefer not to cook, browse through gourmet markets, mail-order catalogs, and culinary websites for a selection of French wines, olive oils, truffles, and other delectable morsels that will add a hint of Gallic flavor to your table.

OPPOSITE: *Sumptuously appointed with toile wallpaper and velvet drapes fringed to match the chair cushions, this dining room sets the stage for fine cuisine. An elaborate chandelier, a gilt-framed oil painting, a grand soup tureen, and a pair of ceramic roosters contribute to the refined look. At first glance, the decor seems best-suited to elegant French porcelain and Baccarat crystal, but one can also envision casual faïence and colorful cut-glass tumblers being equally at home in the milieu.*

◆◆

CHAPTER SEVEN

BEDROOMS
AND BATHS

Taking time to enjoy life's pleasures rather than rushing through them is an essential part of the French country lifestyle. Applying this philosophy to matters of the home requires the creation of inviting retreats—places where residents can slow down and unwind after a long day. The private areas of the home—bedrooms and baths—suit this purpose splendidly, at least when treated the right way. That is, a bathroom should be more than a quick stop in the morning's race to work, and a bedroom should be more than just a place to sleep. Instead, the former should accommodate luxurious bubble baths and well-deserved pampering, while the latter should encourage lounging, reading, quiet contemplation, and plain relaxation. When outfitted according to our favorite indulgences, these spaces can become comforting refuges—safe havens devoted to restoring and nurturing both body and soul. And French country style provides the opportunity to lavish these private escapes with romantic touches.

DREAM ROOMS

Historically speaking, the French country bedroom was hardly the enchanting retreat we picture today. In fact, from the Renaissance to the French Revolution, the king's sleeping chamber was a veritable public place. Louis XIV not only

PAGE 116: *The French have become masters at designing dreamy bedrooms. In this example, floral fabric cascades from a half tester, turning an ordinary bed into a romantic* lit d'ange *(angel's bed). A needlepoint pillow depicting a French château provides a charming finishing touch.*

issued royal edicts from his bedchamber but began each day with a ceremonial rising called a levee, during which privileged guests would watch him don his royal garments and eat breakfast.

For the common folk in the countryside, sleeping spaces had considerably less pomp—and not much more privacy. Until well into the nineteenth century, most of these families slept in the single communal room that made up their dwelling; beds were tucked in a corner near the fire for warmth. What's more, during the winter months in cold areas such as the Alps, the family would share this space with their livestock. Letting sheep sleep under the beds not only protected the animals from the elements but also created the effect of a heated blanket. Even in provincial homes boasting sleeping lofts, family members shared the space, usually with several children tucked in together since beds were costly and families large.

These close quarters led to the development of the canopy bed (*lit à baldaquin*). For those who could afford them, hanging fabrics kept out drafts and dust—and provided a modicum of privacy. The unusual wooden box beds (*lits-clos*) that dominated such damp northern areas as Brittany and Normandy served the same purpose. Charming, though not for the claustrophobic, *lits-clos* are usually enclosed at the top and on all four sides, sometimes with a curtain over the opening.

As a more prosperous middle class gradually emerged in the countryside in the centuries following the French Revolution, rooms were added and loftlike larders refashioned to create cozy refuges for sleeping. Canopies evolved from a pragmatic element to a decorative accent, with myriad variations. Even today, the canopy bed is one of the hallmarks of the French country bedroom.

Fabric is lavished not just on canopies but on nearly every surface. Beds are piled high with fluffy pillows, down comforters, and beautiful quilts,

OPPOSITE: *Box beds* (lits-clos), *which protected occupants from drafts and dust, were favored long ago in the cool regions of Normandy and Brittany. This painted example sports a carved balustrade design that gives the small opening the appearance of a balcony.*

LEFT: *Mounds of plump pillows promise comfort in this delightful French country–style bedroom, which gains its appeal from a rich blend of colors and patterns. Notice how the various shams echo other decorative elements in the room, including the lamp shade, the curtains, the bed skirt, and the quilt.*

wrapping occupants in a feeling of luxury. Not to be outdone, windows host curtains that tumble gracefully from the ceiling and pool at the floor. Chairs are dressed up with plump cushions, and hardwood and tile floors are warmed by rugs. Dainty floral patterns and airy pastel color schemes are favorites, though bolder designs can work equally well.

Some bedrooms become marvelous flights of fancy by being decked out almost entirely in toile. Windows, beds, seating, and even walls can be bathed in these delightful bucolic scenes for a sumptuous look that contrasts wonderfully with such rugged architectural details as slanted ceilings and exposed beams. This combination of romantic sophistication and historic charm gives the bedroom a softness that is unmatched by other areas of the provincial home.

SWEET SLUMBER

The classic French country bedroom that fills an armchair traveler's imagination tends to be a quaint hideaway tucked under the eaves, with dormer windows and a curiously pitched roof—a warm, welcoming haven to collapse into after a long day of exploring the countryside, wandering through open-air markets, and dining at memorable cafés. No wonder many of us long to capture a bit of that magic each night.

To evoke a French country ambience at home, begin with the bed—the room's centerpiece. The first option would be, of course, to incorporate an authentic French country canopy bed—perhaps a *lit à colonnes* (traditional four-poster) hung with curtains or a *lit d'ange* (featuring four short posts, a headboard, and a half tester). You could also take various measures to capture the effect of a canopy with the bed that you already have. To simulate the look of a *lit d'ange*, you could purchase or construct a lightweight wooden box to be covered with fabric and then affixed either to the ceiling over the bed or to the wall above the headboard to create a half tester. Fabric swags should be designed to cascade down either side of the box, emulating the lines of a canopy around the bed. Another option is to affix three short dowels to the wall over the headboard, with one centered high up and the others farther down and wide apart to form a triangle. Then drape a bright cotton print from Provence, a perky toile, a panel of gauzy lace, or another pretty French country fabric over the dowels like a canopy.

OPPOSITE: *The treatment is pure French country, with delicate green-and-white toile de Jouy from stem to stern. Walls, windows, footboard, and even the half tester are covered in toile, while the seating and bedcovers feature color-coordinated fabrics.*

BELOW: *Decorative dowels were positioned above the head of this bed, then draped with scallop-edged fabric to lend the setting a feminine look. The airy canopy is accompanied by a pretty square of antique fabric mounted on the wall to create a novel headboard. For a change of pace, the textiles can easily be replaced with other fabrics.*

But canopy beds are not the only possibilities for a French country bedroom. Two beds that became quite fashionable after the French Revolution and remain fixtures in country homes today are the sleigh bed (*lit en bateau*) and the daybed (*lit de repos*). Both were beloved in the nineteenth century for their simplicity, which was favored in rejection of the old aristocracy's ostentatious tastes. While a sleigh bed, with its massive presence, is better off in a spacious room, daybeds can work miracles in tight quarters. The latter have the ability not only to take up residence in small spaces and nestle under eaves but also to double as seating. This versatility makes them an ideal solution for a guest room that must act as a sitting room or study as well. In general, situating a bed against a wall will make a room seem larger—a strategy that the French discovered while grappling with the small spaces and peculiar angles of old houses. In fact, to reproduce the cozy security of a *lit-clos*, you could arrange a bed against a wall painted rich vermilion, then cover a paneled folding screen in red-and-white toile and place it next to the head or foot of the bed to suggest a private alcove.

Headboards are another means of injecting a French country note into a bedroom. Interior designer Carole Winer, a master at finding ingenious new uses for reclaimed pieces, has transformed numerous antiques into novel headboards. "I've turned pairs of old French doors, decorative iron fences, even panels from *lits-clos* into gorgeous headboards," she says. "They work wonderfully for king-size beds, since true antique kings are very hard to find." Winer has also turned nineteenth-century gilt picture frames into headboards by covering them with upholstery and mounting them on the wall.

BELOW: *Framed by floral-print drapes and situated in a cozy alcove, this bed simulates the protected feeling of a* lit-clos. *The sensation is reinforced by the niche's wallpaper, which features the same design as the curtains and dust ruffle and helps bring the setup's individual components into a seamless whole.*

FURNISHINGS AND FLOURISHES

OPPOSITE: *A rush-seat ladder-back settee and a small painted wooden table provide warm counterpoints to the wrought-iron bed frame. Cushions atop the settee make it a comfortable spot for reading and relaxing, while the diminutive table offers a place to rest a cup of water or a pair of eyeglasses at bedtime.*

After you've settled upon the style of your bed, round out the space with a smattering of well-chosen pieces. French country bedrooms are often furnished with nothing more than a few cherished antiques, perfectly balanced to achieve a sense of restrained simplicity that offsets the abundance of fabrics. Consider outfitting your private retreat with a stylish chest of drawers, a cozy chair or two for reading, and a pair of mismatched nightstands with a different lamp perched atop each one. A distinguished armoire can also make a noteworthy contribution. The primary repository for linens and clothes in ages past, the armoire was also a classic wedding gift for young French brides. Hence, many feature romantic motifs such as inlaid copper doves, once deemed a symbol of true love, and carved baskets of roses. (Tradition held that the number of flowers carved on the surface of a Norman armoire dictated its value.)

Carved and polished woods are quite at home in the provincial bedroom, as are painted finishes and even wrought iron. As in other parts of the French country home, contrasting furniture styles are often mixed to heighten drama and visual interest. An old four-poster bed, its green-and-gold paint slightly cracked and peeling, could pair perfectly with formal gilt-rimmed mirrors. Likewise, a rough-hewn pine armoire, admired for its distressed grain, might complement a cherry sleigh bed polished to a warm, honey-brown glow. Each of these design schemes is unified by the interesting shapes and textures of its components as well as a sense of history.

Once you've chosen furnishings, add the flourishes—perhaps a lovely Aubusson carpet, wallpaper in a similar color scheme, and then a bedspread and dust ruffle to blend. An antiques lover might cap such bed linens with an authentic *boutis* (quilted bedspread). Made from the same colorful printed cotton as the famous *indiennes* and top-stitched for decorative effect, *boutis* were supposedly introduced to Marseilles by the king of Naples in the fifteenth century. As time went on, they became a familiar decorative element in southern French interiors. In fact, for centuries, they were a favorite bridal gift, often embroidered with pomegranates to symbolize fertility.

Like the *boutis* they complement so well, sheets and pillowcases were once a much-treasured wedding gift. Today vintage linens are highly sought as collectibles, and fabulous pieces can be found with hand-stitched initials,

ABOVE: *Incorporating cherished objects collected over the years will make your retreat feel all the more personal. Here, a small table plays host to an antiques lover's treasure trove of wooden jewelry boxes, crystal decanters, and other prized possessions.*

ABOVE: *Toile de Jouy wallpaper featuring dapper rabbits in waistcoats provides a delightful backdrop for a child's room tucked under the eaves. At the center of the space, a fanciful table with carrot legs offers an enticing spot for art projects, games, and make-believe.*

reminders of a bride's trousseau from long ago. Remember, however, that these textiles can be both expensive and fragile. Watch for discoloration and fraying when you shop, since such damage cannot always be mended. Also, bear in mind that antique linens were made for narrower beds than those we use today.

For a classic French country look, you could cover a bedroom entirely in a single fabric—say, a mini-print of peach roses or a vibrant blue-and-yellow toile. In such a design scheme, valances, bedcovers, chairs, and even wallpaper merge to convey a sense of cheerful warmth and to deceive the eye by blurring boundaries.

CHILDREN'S ROOMS

The cheery colors, cozy warmth, and ample whimsy of French country style make it an ideal source of inspiration for children's bedrooms. A little girl's nursery might be covered in a dainty mini-print of roses or delicate pink-and-white toile, for example. A few years later, a canopy bed covered in the same pretty pattern could replace her crib, and a pint-size upholstered rocker could take the place of a changing table skirted in toile. Windows could be covered with a lace or piqué swag or, for a more elaborate look, balloon valances with fabric rosettes in a muted pink-and-yellow plaid.

A little boy's room would look equally charming with a fern green or powder blue toile and tailored, striped cotton curtains in matching hues. Some companies even make toiles featuring little animals in waistcoats and other evocative motifs reminiscent of the illustrations in children's literature.

In fact, books can be a springboard for any number of intriguing themes. Enlist the help of an art student to decorate your child's walls with gaily painted representations of his or her favorite French storybook characters—Madeline, the little Parisian schoolgirl; Tintin, from the popular French cartoon strip; or the Little Prince, from Antoine de Saint-Exupery's classic tale. A figure like Babar the elephant is simple enough that, if you're artistically inclined, you might paint him yourself. Complete the imaginative setting with a few toy versions of the character and, of course, the books themselves.

The possibilities for fun-filled, stimulating rooms abound. You could incorporate a trompe l'oeil mural that lets your child venture away to a sunny harbor full of sailing ships or a countryside dotted with rolling hills and picturesque farmhouses. For a youngster studying the language, lines from a French nursery rhyme could be written in a vibrant shade of paint along a wall at chair-rail height or near the ceiling. If your family possesses a joint French and American heritage, you might celebrate this background by appointing your child's

ABOVE: *A setting befitting two fairy-tale princesses boasts antique twin beds, each given a* baldaquin *treatment with canopies of chestnut fabric edged by cocoa-and-cream toile. These muted tones blend well with the soft fawn walls, subdued rose accents, and gingham dust ruffles. The scene is almost sophisticated enough to tempt adults, yet the corner toy cabinet and the stuffed rabbits dozing on the beds let you know that this is a room meant for little girls to dream in.*

room in bold red, white, and blue. Ring one door frame with stencils of gold fleur-de-lis and another with gold eagles. Finally, share your fondness for French culture by tucking a French folk CD into your child's music collection and looking through picture books of France together.

But you needn't fill a room with an abundance of complicated patterns to conjure a provincial atmosphere. Even the simplest touches can express a remarkable amount of ambience. For a hint of Provençal charm, you might cover a nightstand in a vivid orange-and-yellow cotton print fabric, add a pillow covered in a similar print to an inviting armchair, and then complete the picture with a ceramic vase of sunflowers. If you prefer something more subdued, consider a neutral palette that combines shades of eggshell and farm-fresh cream with tones of chestnut, toasted almond, and mellow brown. In keeping with such a scheme, accents could include antique lace pillow coverings, small

OPPOSITE: *A thoughtful host converted an attic room into hospitable guest quarters. While the configuration of the roof could have been a drawback, it has become the room's best asset, offering protected nooks for two twin beds.*

ABOVE: *A bedroom decorated in a creamy palette receives a dose of French country zest from a Provençal-print textile draped over an occasional table.*

ABOVE: *A roomy window seat makes the most of a stunning bay window. Although toile is sprinkled liberally over the space—used for the cushions, balloon shades, and bed—it is still employed with more restraint than in many French country bedrooms, where it would also be lavished on the walls. Here, a flattering backdrop of burnt sienna has a tempering effect on the profusion of patterns.*

rustic baskets hung on the wall or used to store reading materials near the bed, and a stack of vintage leather suitcases passing as a nightstand. To vary the look for a new season, draw your inspiration from classic chinoiserie and add a sprinkling of Provençal prints and floral fabrics, all in blue and white. Then top them off with a large white ceramic urn filled with dazzling blue hydrangeas. The simple palette works brilliantly to offset busy patterns.

Remember that the bedroom is your private sanctuary, safe from the prying eyes of outsiders. Use your imagination to create a personalized setting that makes you feel comfortable and content the moment you step inside—a space worthy of inspiring only the happiest dreams.

BATHING IN STYLE

In a culture where aesthetics are prized in even the tiniest details and great delight is taken in savoring life's simple joys, it seems only natural that much care and thought be given to one of the home's smallest but most significant rooms: the bath. The French regard this space as a place to luxuriate and indulge the senses. Indeed, bathing leisurely is deemed so preferable to hastily dousing oneself in a shower that a tub is all but de rigueur in French homes. Even today, it is quite common—as anyone who has spent time in rural France knows—to find a bathroom featuring a tub outfitted with a handheld sprayer rather than an actual shower.

Of course, the French didn't always hold bathing in such high regard. In centuries past, the practice was disdained as immodest and even dangerous to one's health. It wasn't until the early twentieth century that residents of the French countryside began to modernize their homes to include a *salle de bain*. As a result, bathrooms are frequently located in erstwhile maids' chambers and other out-of-the-way nooks, which imbues them with a charmingly quirky character.

SOAKING IN AMBIENCE

Bathrooms provide an ideal setting for the glazed, hand-painted tiles so popular in Provence. The signature scheme is a deep sapphire-and-goldenrod design against a bright white background—colors reminiscent of the vivid sea and sun for which the region is famous. However, you might just as successfully borrow a broader interpretation of Mediterranean style and use tiles in a variety of other bold, saturated shades. Complement them with decorative majolica or terra-cotta accents to evoke the vital spirit of that sun-drenched region of Europe. One affordable approach is to install a block of colorful hand-painted tiles in the midst of plainer ones. You could also employ the more lavishly embellished tiles as a border.

To make straightforward tiles more intriguing and to create an illusion of spaciousness, lay them on the diagonal in a diamond pattern. A monochromatic palette or a single pattern spread over every surface will also make a bath appear larger than its physical dimensions. So will a generous use of mirrors—position them strategically to double the impact of noteworthy architectural

BELOW: *Stone tiles arranged in a diamond pattern team up with reproduction antique hardware to bring a bit of old-world elegance to this bathroom. The handheld sprayer substituting for a shower is not uncommon in France, where leisurely baths are preferred over hurried, two-minute showers. Forsythia and ivy add a romantic garden ambience, further tempting visitors to indulge in a bubble bath.*

RIGHT: *The owner has turned a passion for antique mirrors into a unique decorative statement for a top-story bathroom. Not only do the reflective accents create the illusion of added space, they call attention to the interesting architecture. In fact, the large multipaned mirror provides the simple, all-white surroundings with a bonus architectural component, as it is actually a reclaimed window fitted with mirrored glass.*

OPPOSITE: *Who wouldn't be tempted to sink into a warm, fragrant bath in this old-fashioned claw-foot tub, surrounded by such luxuries as polished hardwood floors and a marble fireplace? A tiled inset creates the impression of a rug beneath the tub while offering a practical, waterproof surface. Enhancing the regal feel of the space is a statuesque armoire—an ideal home for piles of plush towels. A room such as this should have plenty of ventilation to help protect the wood from warping.*

features and eye-catching details, such as a stripped and polished wooden window frame decked with a pretty French country fabric sash.

Any bathroom that hopes to capture the spirit of the French countryside should include a tub if at all possible—a place to unwind, close your eyes, and soak in soothing warm water. Claw-foot versions are well loved in France for their nostalgic charm, as are antique faucets. The latter often include interesting forms, such as hot- and cold-water controls crafted to resemble fish or whales.

Reproduction or reclaimed antique sinks and tubs will add an old-world flair to a bath. If you do not wish to invest in such fixtures, you could take some creative strategies to beautify the amenities that you already have. For

BELOW: *This farmhouse's ancient ceiling beams are still visible, and the original multipaned windows have been left in place to usher in afternoon breezes and sunshine. But you don't need to live in a centuries-old home to enjoy these kinds of architectural delights. Such details can be reclaimed and added to a modern home to immerse it in historic charm.*

instance, exposed pipes beneath a basin might be concealed by shirring a sunny Provençal fabric on a rod around the base of the sink. Or hire a carpenter to construct a wooden cabinet frame to enclose the sink's base, and have matching wood panels built to frame the sides of an unattractive tub for an unfitted look. Leave the wood exposed to achieve a rustic feel, or paint it a favorite color. An old cast-iron tub that has seen better days might become a showpiece with a simple makeover of paint and swirling grapevines or rippling waves stenciled along its sides.

To give the bathroom an aura of history and age befitting a venerable country house, nothing works better than the look of antique furnishings. A

LEFT: *A magnificent trompe l'oeil mural whisks bathers away to an enchanting estate in the countryside. The magical scene not only has a soothing effect but also opens up the room.*

stately cherry armoire—real or reproduction—might be loaded with fluffy towels and washcloths. For a more carefree mood, a dilapidated old ladder-back chair freshened up with a coat of turquoise paint could hold towels at the ready. If you hope to include wood in your decor, make sure that the room has ample ventilation, and avoid rare or costly pieces, as humidity may warp them over time.

For those with a romantic soul, France's fabled country gardens might give rise to a lush retreat overgrown with plants. Reinforce the motif with botanical murals, prints of Monet's famous water-lily canvases, or authentic wrought-iron garden accents. A rectangular iron planter filled with multicolored towels, all neatly rolled to resemble blossoming flowers, makes a delightful touch. Even an interesting lattice or old garden gate can find new life as a sculptural accent for an unused wall.

RIGHT: *Toile works just as well in the bath as in other rooms of the French country home. Here, black-and-white pastoral scenes add a dramatic flourish to deep russet walls and hardwood floors. Note how placing tiles on the diagonal inside a decorative black border has transformed an ordinary shower wall into something special.*

OPPOSITE: *Often it is the tiniest details that make the strongest statement in a bath. Time and effort went into collecting the old-style shaving accessories, fine hand-milled French soap, fresh lavender, and pretty containers that form this pleasing vignette. Above the vanity, a painted tree branch ambles through the scene, adding interest to an understated wall. Below the sink, French bath products are neatly stashed in labeled boxes.*

Another tactic is to draw inspiration from the vivid colors and patterns that work so well elsewhere in French provincial design. Following this path, you could fill the bathroom with valances and shower curtains decked in bright stripes, checks, or toiles. Reinforce the glorious colors with warm lighting—sconces, soft bulbs in overhead lights, or perhaps a chandelier for a dramatic statement.

Personalized collections, too, can find a home in the bath as easily as in any other room. Antique apothecary jars might hold bath salts, for example, while charming old French tobacco tins offer a convenient spot in which to stash cotton balls and swabs.

ABOVE, LEFT AND RIGHT: *The claw-foot tub gives this bathroom an old-style European flavor, while the bath oils on the sink counter and beside the tub provide a distinctly French touch. Fresh-cut hydrangeas bring a hint of the countryside indoors.*

If you favor a conservative approach, bring just a few splashes of French country style into an otherwise understated bath. Red-and-white toile fingertip towels, hand-milled French vanilla soaps, and a Limoges bud vase holding a scarlet rose will make an all-white, ivory, or taupe powder room festive at Christmastime. When spring breezes return, these decorative elements can be replaced by pale purple and yellow towels and scented soaps in the same pastel shades.

PAMPERING PLEASURES

To fully appreciate the delights of the bath, you will need a few of France's marvelous *produits de bain* to tempt the nose and soothe the skin. Chunky, rough-carved blocks of *savon de Marseilles,* the city's world-famous olive oil–based soaps, might grace the edge of the tub. Or perhaps you would prefer seaweed-infused exfoliating bars from the Breton coast. Fill a porcelain dish or line a shelf with an assortment of silky *huiles de bain* (bath oils), gels that bubble into rich lather, invigorating face cleansers, delicate powders, and satiny body lotions—all laced with such deliciously heady fragrances as jasmine, rosemary, orange, and lavender.

Heighten the ambience by including a basket of potpourri, a few beeswax candles, and plenty of irresistibly soft, cuddly Egyptian cotton towels. Finally, set aside time to luxuriate in a bath that will leave you as refreshed and rejuvenated as if you had slipped away to the French countryside for a brief vacation.

♦♦

CHAPTER EIGHT

OUTDOOR SPACES

Proof of the French passion for gardening is evident in many aspects of the culture, from the village markets filled with ripe vegetables and fresh-cut flowers to the beloved canvases of Impressionists Claude Monet and Auguste Renoir. Dutch-born artist Vincent van Gogh found himself so enraptured by the country gardens of Provence, where he went to paint in the late nineteenth century, that he raved about the enormous red roses and fig trees, comparing their beauty to poetry.

Gardens even find their way *inside* French country homes in the form of fabrics and furnishings adorned with fruit and flower motifs. Toiles celebrate bucolic pastimes with images of aristocrats reposing on garden swings or under trellises entwined with green ivy. Chintz is strewn with romantically meandering vines, bright blossoms, and clusters of ripe berries. Provençal cottons are emblazoned with majestic sunflowers, neat rows of tiny roses, and other uplifting flower, fruit, and vegetable designs. Even armoires and buffets are carved and painted with lavish bouquets, while dining tables are dressed up with pitchers of cut flowers and laden with a cornucopia of garden-fresh ingredients that change with every season.

The deep love of the soil and the outdoors that exists among residents of rural France stems in part from a long tradition of farming, harvesting grapes, and other agricultural pursuits. Good weather is seldom wasted with a meal

PAGE 140: *Simple garden furniture is set under a massive shade tree, inviting visitors to enjoy a pleasant afternoon respite on the grounds of the stately manor house. In rural France, where much of the population has been involved in agricultural pursuits over the centuries, there is a great love of the outdoors.*

RIGHT: *Floral carpeting, a wicker chaise longue, and an abundance of potted plants create the feeling of a lush garden in this charming sunroom. A magnificent antique finch cage provides a focal point at one end of the space, where it sits atop a large table draped in a plaid textile. Strategically placed lighting calls attention to a trio of plant-filled faïence vessels, while a trail of verdant ivy crowns a pair of French doors.*

OPPOSITE: *Plein air dining provides a delightful way to capture the spirit of French country living. Blossoms freshly picked from the garden brighten each plate at this rustic table, which has been dressed up with linens, crystal, and colorful china. Note how each dinner plate features the same pattern but a different color, thereby giving each guest an air of distinction while maintaining a sense of harmony.*

inside when one could picnic in the garden or enjoy an alfresco lunch on the patio. Outdoor areas are often skillfully converted into lush hideaways where oleander and geraniums overflow terra-cotta pots, and wisteria vines, heavy with purple blossoms, clamber up old brick and stucco walls. Streetside, doorways framed with leafy climbers and windowsills brimming with red, yellow, and blue flowers hint at the charming gardens hidden behind cottage gates and farmhouse walls.

Why not cultivate a tranquil retreat of your own where you can indulge in the heady fragrances of flowers and herbs, rejuvenate your spirit with a favorite book, or enjoy a plein air dinner with friends? Gardens and patios provide a wonderful way to honor the relaxed, casual lifestyle of the French countryside. Moreover, tilling the earth and nurturing plants offers a tactile way to connect with the agrarian soul of French provincial culture.

VISUAL FEASTS

Unlike the well-manicured, neatly geometric *jardins à la française* of Versailles and other châteaux, gardens belonging to typical provincial dwellings exude a looser, more casual kind of charm. In addition to plants sprouting up from the ground, these verdant retreats often boast vibrantly glazed ceramic pots bearing even more vibrant flowers. Every corner and crevice blossoms, with flora suspended from wrought-iron plant hangers affixed to walls and fence posts at every conceivable height. Fruit trees, herbs, flowers, and vegetables crowd together in a boisterous jumble. The result is a kaleidoscope of brilliant hues and fascinating textures. The Riviera's subtropical climate gives rise to dazzling hibiscus, bougainvillea, spiky acanthus, and citrus trees clustered in gardens edged by laurel and box hedges. Meanwhile, in coastal Normandy, hydrangea and azalea bushes might share space with purple phlox and wild cherry trees. In Grasse, a garden might pay tribute to the city's renowned perfume industry with a fragrant blend of roses, jasmine, and honeysuckle.

RIGHT: *This picturesque cottage seems to be in full bloom, thanks to the flower bed, rose-covered pergola, and container plantings. The French expertise at growing things in small spaces often results in multiple levels of greenery and blossoms.*

OPPOSITE: *From the container garden abutting the house and the flower beds encircling the trees to the informal bouquets on the table, an abundance of blooms enhances the outdoor dining experience. Shades of lavender and rose accenting the furnishings echo nature's palette.*

ABOVE, LEFT: *Rotund containers glazed in the mustard yellow and sage green so characteristic of Provence are filled with hot peppers, begonias, and herbs. Cheerful glazed earthenware cachepots are adept at lending a French country flair to both interior and exterior spaces. Small versions work well for a picnic table, particularly when paired with plates boasting a coordinating color scheme or pattern.*

ABOVE, RIGHT: *Sheltered from the sun, a slatted chair and matching table create a cool spot for a relaxing breakfast. In the background, humble clay pots filled with hardy pink and white geraniums heighten the beauty of the setting.*

The French—like residents of many other parts of Europe—are masters at bringing bountiful gardens to life in the tiniest of spaces. In arid southern France, this expertise arose through necessity. With rain scarce, rich soil was limited and had to be reserved for crops, which provided sustenance and a livelihood. Those yearning for the beauty of flowering plants and the culinary benefits of herbs soon became adept at nurturing small specimens in pots that could easily be tended and watered.

Many homes in southern France boast a garden almost entirely composed of flower-filled clay pots and wrought-iron planters. You might re-create the look by collecting an interesting assortment of containers and filling them with exuberant crimson and snowy white geraniums, to be lavished over every ledge and small table. Nearby, terra-cotta pots filled with stalks of narcissus or clusters of impatiens could punctuate each level in a series of garden steps.

GARDENING INDOORS

Taking a cue from the French, who know that many an unlikely space can blossom into a verdant garden, you can easily cultivate a feeling of lush vegetation *inside* your home. This is a practical strategy for those who live in apartments, lack large yards, or simply wish to enhance their interiors with the cheerful freshness of flowering plants.

The first step is to go to a nursery and inquire as to what types of plants will work in your home. Find out what varieties are likely to thrive based on the direction your windows face (this affects the intensity of light the plants will receive) and the amount of humidity in your residence. With central heating, air tends to become dry in the winter, so it may be necessary to mist plants, use moisture-retaining pots and potting techniques, or purchase a small, inexpensive humidifier. Ask how much water the plants you are interested in need, if they require pruning, and whether they are perennials or annuals, the latter surviving only one season.

It's also wise to inquire about the fragrances of various flowering plants before investing in them. Many blossoms exude a distinctive scent, from the light, whispery sweetness of miniature cyclamen to the heady, pungent perfume of hyacinths and gardenias. Filling a room with the aromas of orange blossom and lavender can enhance your home's garden ambience and inspire fond memories of your favorite vacation spot on the Riviera. Conversely, you may discover too late that the scent of a beautiful bloom overpowers your living room.

Before you purchase any plants, make sure you have an appropriate place to put them. You'll need a spot where they'll be able to receive the appropriate amount of sunlight. You'll also want a location that is easily accessible so that caring for them does not become an uncomfortable chore. Last but not least, the plants should be situated so that you can admire and enjoy them often. You might purchase a tiered, wrought-iron plant stand and set pots on each level to create a pyramid of green ivy under a living room window. Or you could fill a dining room windowsill with bright yellow

ABOVE: *This kitchen's windowsill garden keeps fresh seasonings at the ready for the chef.*

begonias and primroses in blue-and-white china cachepots to complement yellow-and-blue chinoiserie wallpaper. If you want something with a more practical bent, you could go with an assortment of tiny terra-cotta pots bearing chives, sage, and other cooking herbs—a lovely accent for a sunny kitchen counter.

Once you've decided what types of plants to purchase and where to put them, add a bit of French country flair with interesting pots and decorative techniques. Glazed ceramic bowls and terra-cotta pots will bring a touch of provincial beauty to any interior. For a farmhouse flavor, call upon old tin garden buckets, distressed stone urns, or antique faïence pitchers to act as flowerpots. To create an eye-catching vignette, line a mantel with frothy green helxine punctuated by vintage crockery creamers packed with dried flowers. As a finishing touch, supplement your real-life blooms with a framed French botanical print or a classic French Impressionist tableau such as Renoir's *A Girl with a Watering Can*.

RIGHT: *A field of lavender is one of the images that springs to mind when thinking about Provence. Here, rows of the fragrant herb are joined by an array of bright blooms, creating a mesmerizing display of color and pattern.*

The charming, eclectic quality that permeates French country interiors extends to outdoor areas as well, affecting not only garden ornaments and hardscape elements but the plantings themselves. Old distressed wooden benches and chipped stone urns in subdued earthy hues take up residence next to newly glazed ceramic pots filled with blue delphinium, purple bougainvillea, orange hibiscus, and pink petunias. This visual potpourri yields a richer, more dramatic effect than that of a garden planted exclusively with coordinated colors and textures. The resulting mélange, which echoes the countless shapes and hues of flowers growing in the wild, is also more reflective of the way in which Nature herself works when left to her own devices.

If you are a novice and have limited time to devote to your garden, visit a local garden center, call a nearby garden club, or obtain the name of a master gardener from your state's agricultural extension service. All three sources should be able to offer helpful advice, free of charge, about what flowers will likely grow best with minimal care, given the local climate and the amount of light in your yard. It's also wise to inquire about composting, fertilizer, and other means of enriching the soil. If you would like your garden to offer a continuous display of color, ask for help selecting a range of plants that will bloom at different times over the spring, summer, and fall. Consider planting a few perennials (bright orange daylilies, buttery daffodils, and purple tulips, for example) to produce favorite flowers year after year, then supplement them with newcomers each spring.

While lavender and sunflowers are the undisputed signatures of Provence and roses and geraniums are favorites in the north, French soil is home to seemingly countless choices that are sure to delight the gardener. Rather than attempt to find flowers that look specifically French to you, select ones that strike your fancy and are capable of thriving in your particular location. Then develop a provincial flavor through decorative accents and arrangement.

For those in search of an authentically French garden, a *potager* is a splendid option. These little kitchen gardens, so beloved in France, feature tomatoes, leeks, lettuces, onions, and other vegetables, as well as aromatic herbs. Among the most common are basil, savory, sage, thyme, mint, and oregano. Planted in small flower beds or individual pots, they offer a unique opportunity to enjoy the changing seasons via fresh-from-the-garden ingredients for your table.

GARDEN ACCENTS

One of the most imaginative ways to enliven a garden is through interesting accents, such as antique garden tools—popular collectibles in both France and the United States. Like flowers, these elements needn't come from France. If you have access to a flea market near your home, look for vintage plant holders, spades, hoes, or shovels. A bit of rust and dirt will only enhance the character of these garden implements and add to their rustic, distressed charm. A collection of antique watering cans fashioned from copper or metal—some squat and plump, others slender and graceful—will make a striking statement placed along

a ledge. Likewise, an old weathervane or metal birdcage will add interest to a flower bed. Though prices for antique garden items vary tremendously in the United States and France, affordable pieces are readily available.

If you have a large garden or yard, you might take the more elaborate approach of incorporating wrought-iron or stone antiques salvaged from gardens in France. Trellises, sundials, pedestals, statues, busts, urns, and even outdoor furnishings may be purchased from salvage companies that specialize in finding unusual architectural accents in France and bringing them to other countries. Though these elements can be costly and difficult to transport because of their size and weight, such finds make one-of-a-kind showpieces in a garden. For a grand flourish, you might make a centerpiece of an old fountain that once provided drinking water in a French village square. Interior designer Carole Winer often uses antique wrought-iron arcs called *gloriettes* to create gazebos for her clients. "They come in all sorts of shapes and sizes, and when you plant them with wisteria or ivy, it will grow over the top so that you'll have a beautiful spot for a settee or a bench inside," she says. For a simpler, more whimsical approach,

RIGHT: *On a porch outfitted with various country furnishings and accents, a simple wooden sign bidding visitors* bienvenue *(welcome) contributes a specifically French note.*

hang an old French street sign from a garden wall or put a beaded curtain across the doorway that leads from the house to the garden. The latter—a clever trick used to let air flow through an open doorway while keeping insects out—is popular in southern France.

Gardens and patios are also perfect homes for the hand-painted and terra-cotta tiles beloved throughout the Mediterranean. Decorative tile borders often adorn garden walls, steps, and patio edges, adding a splash of dazzling color that is reinforced by glazed pots in complementary hues. A pair of bright blue pots

brimming with yellow petunias makes a cheerful greeting at the beginning of a garden path lined with tiles in cheery Provençal yellow, blue, and white. For a more delicate approach, pale celery-toned tiles pair well with pots of the same pale green filled with bold red geraniums. Be sure to use only tiles originally designed for outdoor use. Doug Karlson, president of Country Floors, also cautions that if you live in a climate where temperatures drop below freezing in the winter, you should avoid terra-cotta, which is apt to crack and flake in such weather.

Give your garden or patio the ability to function as a hospitable outdoor room by adding furnishings that will encourage you to actually use and enjoy the space. Place a small wrought-iron table and chairs in a convenient spot, set a rustic bench at the edge of the garden where you can admire your handiwork, or collect slightly scuffed versions of the green-painted folding chairs that are fixtures in Parisian parks. The folding chairs are lightweight, making them easily portable for those on a quest for the sunniest or shadiest spots.

The advantage of a table, of course, is that it encourages you to enjoy outdoor meals. Don't restrict yourself to paper plates and plastic cups. There's no reason you can't bring everyday wineglasses or colorful cut-glass tumblers

ABOVE, LEFT: *A generously sized white wicker table and comfortable matching chairs invite residents to dine and entertain outdoors. Hanging baskets and other flower-filled containers bring the garden right up to the house.*

ABOVE, RIGHT: *A well-worn tin bucket and brilliant yellow milk pitchers emblazoned with the* Vache qui Rit *(laughing cow) cheese logo play host to radiant bouquets of marigolds. The napkins and dishware feature the same jubilant color scheme, while the tablecloth sports muted versions of the hues.*

outdoors. Colorful faïence plates and bowls also look lovely in an outdoor setting, as do gingham napkins and place mats or Provençal-print tablecloths.

Once you have taken care of the accoutrements, take the time to enjoy brunches, lunches, and dinners in your outdoor room. Simple salads, sandwiches, and traditional grilled fare work well for alfresco meals, as do chilled seafood salads, cold soups, and ratatouille.

Garden settings are also perfect for playing a game of checkers or reading a favorite book. In fact, these simple pleasures become even more enjoyable in the fresh air, particularly on a warm weekend afternoon amid light breezes and the drone of honeybees flitting from blossom to blossom. Of course, you needn't plan an organized activity at all. A simple respite in the garden can be just as delightful. With a glass of chilled chardonnay and the enveloping scents of lavender, pine, and roses, you need only close your eyes to believe you've been whisked away to a blissful garden in the French countryside.

SOURCE DIRECTORY

The following selected guide, which includes the contact information for the companies and shops mentioned in the text of this book, is provided to help you decorate your home in the French country style. Sources are listed alphabetically within specific categories. In cases where numerous stores exist, four locations in various geographic regions have been included along with information regarding how to locate others closer to your residence. This is by no means intended as a comprehensive list. You can find fine French country products through numerous additional sources, from large department stores to individual boutiques and companies offering merchandise exclusively online.

ANTIQUES

Country Loft Antiques
557 Main Street South
Woodbury, CT
203-266-4500

Wirthmore Antiques
3900 Magazine Street
New Orleans, LA
504-899-3811

3727 Magazine Street
New Orleans, LA
504-269-0660
www.wirthmoreantiques.com

ARCHITECTURAL ELEMENTS

Salvage One Architectural Artifacts
1840 West Hubbard
Chicago, IL
312-733-0098
www.salvageone.com

Architectural Salvage, W.D., Inc.
614–618 East Broadway
Louisville, KY
502-589-0670
www.architecturalsalvage.com
Specializes in items for the garden.

BED AND BATH

See also French Country Living, Rue de France, Pierre Deux, and Souleiado shops listed in the "Fabrics, Furnishings, and Home Decor" section.

Yves Delorme
To order a catalog, inquire about other additional store locations, or find stores near you carrying Yves Delorme products, go to www.yvesdelorme.com.

9632 Santa Monica Boulevard
Beverly Hills, CA
310-550-7797

4300 Paces Ferry Road
Atlanta, GA
770-438-7100

10751 Falls Road
Green Spring Station
Baltimore, MD
410-828-4777

442 Depot Street
Manchester Center, VT
802-366-4974

FLOORING AND TILES

Country Floors
15 East 16th Street
New York, NY
212-627-8300

8735 Melrose Avenue
Los Angeles, CA
310-657-0510

Paris Ceramics
To find additional store locations, call 888-845-3487.

150 East 58th Street
New York, NY
212-644-2782

The Merchandise Mart, Suite 1373
Chicago, IL
312-467-9830

205 Seaview Avenue
Palm Beach, FL
561-835-8875

8373 Melrose Avenue
Los Angeles, CA
323-658-8570

KITCHEN AND TABLE

See also French Country Living, Rue de France, Pierre Deux, and Souleiado shops listed in the "Fabrics, Furnishings, and Home Decor" section.

Baccarat *(crystal)*
To inquire about additional store locations or stores carrying Baccarat, call 800-777-0100.

625 Madison Avenue
New York, NY
212-826-4100

238 Greenwich Avenue
Greenwich, CT
888-259-9947

13350 North Dallas Parkway
Suite 1295
Dallas, TX
877-853-2928

343 Powell Street
San Francisco, CA
415-291-0600

Quimper Faïence
To order a catalog, inquire about additional store locations, or find additional stores carrying Quimper Faïence, call 800-470-7339.

141 Water Street
Stonington, CT
860-535-1515

1121 King Street
Alexandria, VA
703-519-8339

Sur La Table
To order a catalog or inquire about additional store locations, call 800-243-0852 or go to www.surlatable.com. For information on Sur La Table cooking classes in Manhasset, New York, call 516-365-3297.

50–54 East Walton Street
Chicago, IL
312-337-0600

5211 Wisconsin Avenue NW
Washington, D.C.
202-237-0375

6333 West Third Street
Los Angeles, CA
323-954-9190

1468 Northern Boulevard
Manhasset, NY
516-365-3297

FABRIC, FURNITURE, AND HOME DECOR

Brunschwig & Fils
Products can be obtained only through a qualified interior designer. To find out more, call 800-538-1880 or go to www.brunschwig.com.

French Country Living
To order a catalog, call 800-485-1302 or go to www.frenchcountryliving.com.

Retail shop:
10135 Colvin Run Road
Great Falls, VA
703-759-2245

Pierre Deux
To order a catalog or find additional store locations, call 888-PIERRE-2. Les Olivades products are available in the United States through Pierre Deux stores.

111 Newbury Street
Boston, MA
617-536-6364

415 Decorative Center
Dallas, TX
214-749-7775

870 Madison Avenue
New York, NY
212-570-9343

134 Maiden Lane
San Francisco, CA
415-296-9940

Rue de France
To order a catalog, call 800-777-0998 or go to www.ruedefrance.com.

Rue de France Retail Store
78 Thames Street
Newport, RI
401-846-3636

Rue de France Outlet Store
3001 East Main Road
Portsmouth, RI
401-682-1505

Souleiado
102-A Main Street
Northeast Harbor, ME
207-276-3828
888-855-2828
www.souleiadousa.com

Souleiado—A French Country Living Shop
87 West Street
Chagrin Falls, OH
440-247-8494
www.souleiadoshop.com

Souleiado/En Provence Inc.
20 Hazelton Avenue
Toronto, Ontario
Canada
416-975-9400

TOURS

Art & Architectural Tours
2715 Valencia Drive
Sarasota, FL
941-365-5214
800-240-1194
www.art-architecttours.com

FURTHER READING

The following volumes proved useful in researching this book and may be of interest to those wanting to find out more about French provincial life and style.

Baudot, François, and Jean Demachy. *Elle Decor: The Grand Book of French Style*. Boston: Little, Brown & Co., 2001.

Brédif, Josette. *Classic Printed Textiles from France, 1760–1843*. London: Thames and Hudson, 1989.

Clemente, Maribeth. *The Riches of France: A Shopping and Touring Guide to the French Provinces*. New York: St. Martin's Griffin, 1997.

Girouard, Mark. *Life in the French Country House*. New York: Alfred A. Knopf, 2000.

Jones, Claire. *Monet's Table: The Cooking Journals of Claude Monet*. New York: Simon and Schuster, 1989.

Kraatz, Anne. *Lace: History and Fashion*. London: Thames and Hudson, 1988.

Lubell, Cecil, ed. *Textile Collections of the World, Vol. 3, France*. New York: Van Nostrand Reinhold Company, 1977.

MacLachlan, Cheryl. *Bringing It Home France*. New York: Clarkson Potter, 1995.

Moulin, Pierre, Pierre LeVec, and Linda Dannenberg. *Pierre Deux's French Country*. New York: Clarkson Potter, 1984.

Price, Sandy. *Exploring the Flea Markets of France*. New York: Three Rivers Press, 1999.

Ruddy, Robin. *French Provincial Furniture*. Atglen, Penn.: Schiffer Publishing, 1998.

Schoeser, Mary. *French Textiles: From 1760 to the Present*. North Pomfret, Vt.: Trafalgar Square, 1992.

Stoeltie, Barbara, and Rene Stoeltie. *Country Houses of France*. New York: Taschen America, LLC, 1999.

Walshe, Paul, and John Miller. *French Farmhouses and Cottages*. London: Weidenfeld & Nicolson, Ltd., 1996.

Weber, Eugen. *Peasants into Frenchmen: The Modernization of Rural France, 1870–1914*. Stanford, Calif.: Stanford University Press, 1976.

PHOTO CREDITS

Arcaid: ©Simon Kenny/Belle, 133 (Stylist: Nadine Bush)

©Daniel Aubry: 26 (Chateau: La Veirerie which is open as a guest house is owned by The Vogue family)

Beateworks/www.beateworks.com: ©Tim Street Porter, 43 right

Brunschwig & Fils: 6, 39, 46, 47, 76–77, 102

Country Loft Antiques: ©Michael Partenio (Interior Design: Carole A. Winer, Woodbury, CT), 54, 55 (Antiques: Country Loft Antiques), 80, 81 (Tile: Country Floors, New York), 90 (Wine-related antiques and accoutrements: Country Loft Antiques); ©William Seitz, 53, 142 bottom (Interior Design: Carole A. Winer, Woodbury, CT)

Edifice: ©Gillian Darley, 21; ©Kim Sayer, 25 bottom

©Phillip Ennis: 120 (Interior Design: Barbara Ostrom & Associates), 131 (Interior Design: Interior Consultants/Denise Balassi)

Estock Photo: ©Simon Harris, 22

©F & E Schmidt Photography: 107 left, 107 right

Folio, Inc: ©Mark Segal, 16–17; ©Catherine Ursillo, 10, 20

French Country Living: ©Astorino Photography, 34 (Stylist: Sharon Duffy), 100, 112, 139, 146 left (Stylist: Sharon Duffy); ©Sylvestro

Photography, 58 (Stylist: Sharon Duffy), 66 right, 75 left, 110 (Stylist: Sharon Duffy), 119 (Stylist: Sharon Duffy)

©Tria Giovan: 116

©Gross & Daley: 135

Interior Archive: ©Tim Beddow, 28; ©Fritz von der Schlenburg, 11, 69, 151

©David Livingston/ www.davidduncanlivingston.com: 89, 105

©Mark Lohman: 2, (Interior Design: Lynn Pries), 44, 45 (Interior Design: Debra Jones), 62 (Interior Design: Barclay Butera), 82, 83 (Interior Design: Lynn Pries, 114 (Interior Design: Janet Lohman), 130, 136 (Interior Design: Penny Bianchi), 138 left, 138 right (Interior Design: Lynn Pries), 153 left, 153 right (Stylist: Sunday Hendrickson)

©Kit Morris/www.kitmorris.com: 85, 147 (Stylist: Liz Ross www.re-design.ws, Home of Caroline and Michael Bailey)

©Keith Scott Morton: 122

On Location: ©Patrick Smith, 29, 70 left, 88 left, 104; ©Guilles Trillard, 56, 125

©David Phelps/david@ davidphelpsphotography.com: 7, 50, 51, 64, 68, 74 (Interior Design: Linda Chase), 99 left (Interior Design: Bo Niles)

©Tim Street Porter: 151 (Interior Design: Annie Kelly)

Positive Images: ©Patricia J. Bruno (stylist): 3, 70 right, 75 right, 111 bottom

Red Cover: ©Christopher Drake, 52, 57 left, 98 (Designer: Julie Prisca), 150 (Designer: Julie Prisca); ©Andreas von Einsiedel, 66 left, 99 right; ©Reto Guntli, 105; ©Brian Harrison, 31, 32, 33, 96, 97, 106, 121, 124; ©Ken Hayden, 37 (Architect/Designer: Andrzej Zarzycki of Collet Zarzycki), 134 (Architect/Designer: Andrzej Zarzycki of Collect Zarzycki), 155 (Architect/Designer: Andrzej Zarzycki of Collet Zarzycki); ©James Kerr, 128, 132; ©Andrew Twort, 123

©Emily Minton Redfield: 67 (Interior Designer: Mary McWilliams and Stephanie Weaver with Stephen Fuller Interiors, Atlanta, GA) 92 (Interior Designer: Carol Weaks, Atlanta, GA), 94 (Interior Designer: Paige Baten, Dallas, TX), 108 (Interior Designer: Suzanne Kasler, Atlanta, GA), 127 (Interior Designer: Liz Williams, Atlanta, GA)

Rue de France: ©Michael Lutch Photography, 40 (Art Direction: Kathy Heydt; Stylist: Judy Selednik)

©Ianthe Ruthven: 118

©Samu Studios/ www.samustudios.com: ©Lee Najman, 14

©Claudio Santini: 101 (Interior Design: Linda Applewhite & Associates/www.applewhite.com)

Scope: ©Michel Guillard, 23 top

©Brad Simmons: 12, 13, 86, 87 bottom (Interior Design: Carrie Warner/Interiors By Design, Inc., Breckenridge, CO, Stylist: Joetta Moulden/Shelterstyle.com), 126

Superstock: 8

©Dominique Vorillon: 18, 48, 60, 137, 140 (Architect/Designer: Gerard Faivre), 152 (Interior Design: Chantal Cloutier)

©Jessie Walker: 27, 38 (Stylist: Aurelia Joyce Pace; Fabrics: Pierre Deux, Inc.), 43 left (Artists: Laura Chappell and Barb Fisher, Denver, CO), 57 right (Stylist: Aurelia Joyce Pace), 84 left (Interior Design: Janice Russillo Designs, Lake Forest, IL; Cabinet Artist: Donna Worth Koda; Floor Finish: Newport Custom Finishes), 84 right (Interior Design: Donna Aylesworth, Chicago, IL), 88 right (Interior Design: Jeanne Goss; Stylist: Aurelia Joyce Pace), 91 (Interior Design: Aurelia Joyce Pace; Collection: Teresa Dodge, CO), 111 top, 113, 129 (Stylist: Aurelia Joyce Pace; Fabrics: Pierre Deux, Inc.), 142 top

Elizabeth Whiting Associates: 24, 25 top, 36, 42, 65, 71, 73, 78, 87 top right, 143, 144, 145, 146 right, 148

©Kat Wolfe: 23 bottom

INDEX